500

WAYS TO GET MORE PEOPLE TO GIVE YOU MORE MONEY!

(And Keep Giving It To You)

T.J. ROHLEDER
Author of *RUTHLESS MARKETING*

Also by T.J. Rohleder:

The Blue Jeans Millionaire
How to Turn Your Kitchen or Spare Bedroom into a Cash Machine
The Black Book of Marketing Secrets (Series)
The Ruthless Marketing Attack
How to Get Super Rich in the Opportunity Market
Five Secrets That Will Triple Your Profits
Ruthless Copywriting Strategies
Ruthless Marketing
50 in 50
Secrets of the Blue Jeans Millionaire
How to Make Millions Sitting on Your Ass!
Foolproof Secrets of Successful Marketers

Printed in the United States of America.
For information address:
Club-20 International • 305 East Main Street • Goessel, KS 67053-0198

Cover and book interior designed by Mary K. Jones

FIRST EDITION

ISBN 978-1-933356-33-4

INTRODUCTION:

Here Are 500 Proven Ways To Get More People To Give You Even More of Their Money...

And then keep giving it to you!

This unique book was written to help you dream up all kinds of newer and better ways to make more money in your business. It will help you work **'on'** your business and not **'in'** it.

This requires more thought than action. It requires you to THINK BIGGER. It also means you have to change your thinking and see your business in an entirely different way... For example, it means thinking about your business through the eyes of all of the people who are most important to its ultimate success: Your customers, staff members, business partners, suppliers, your customers, and your prospective buyers who have never done business with you. Your goal is to sit around and try to figure out as many ways as you can to give all of these people the things they want the most so they will give you the things that you want the most. It also requires you to think like a marketer and get really good at doing all of the things to attract and retain the largest percentage of the best customers in your target market.

Seems so simple, doesn't it?

Well it is simple. But it's never easy.

In fact, in today's overcrowded marketplace, doing all of the things I just mentioned is getting harder all the time. <u>Don't</u> <u>let</u> <u>that</u> <u>fact</u> <u>discourage you</u>. All you have to do is think bigger... think differently... and think even more! Sometimes you're thinking on your feet, and other

3

times you're doing it on your butt… But however you do it — the key to achieving your greatest success in business is TO DO MORE OF IT. Do this and…

The more time you spend working 'on' it and not 'in' it — the more money you'll make!

Does that excite you?

If so — good! Building your business is exciting! **So many books on business and marketing are boring as mud!** The authors are trying hard to show off and prove they know so much more than you do. They make everything way too complicated and confusing — they throw around big words to prove they're smarter than you are… they talk down to you… and what's more, many of the ideas they give you suck! You must dig through the entire book to get a few good ideas that you can use to make more money in your business.

This book is different.

You won't find too many big words or fancy language in this book. There are no confusing theories or overly complicated concepts… I'm definitely not trying to show off and pretend that I know so much more than you do. Instead, what you will get are simple business and marketing ideas that I use to bring in millions of dollars a year in my own businesses. These ideas work! They have brought in many millions for the companies that I have started or been part of and they can do the same for you. I don't care how much money you want to bring in, you can do it with the simple strategies and methods in this book. As you'll see, everything I have to teach you is simple to understand and easy to put into action.

So, why the crazy layout?

This book contains THE VERY BEST from a series of small books I wrote called, "The Little Black Books Of Marketing Secrets." Those books (which were edited and compiled by Chris Bergquist) are laid out

4

like quote books that are easy to skim through. At the current time, there are 18 small volumes in the complete series. The problem is: it's hard to go through all of these little books to find the best ideas — SO I DECIDED TO SOLVE THIS PROBLEM FOR YOU! *Here's how:* my graphic artist Mary Jones and I went through all 18 of these little books to find the best of the best of the tips, tricks, and strategies from each one. And then Mary re-laid out all the pages to make this book more fun to skim through.

Just spend a little time going through this book every day and...

You Will Gain A Genuine, Unfair Advantage Over All Of Your Biggest Competitors!

Does that sound too good to be true? Maybe. But it's not. *Here's why:* Most small business people are working way too hard for too little money. They are trying to wear all the hats... They're too busy working in their business instead of working on it. And finally, they are terrible marketers because they spend VERY LITTLE TIME AND ENERGY thinking through all of the ways to attract and retain the very best customers. They simply do not understand the basic principles of marketing and because of that they have never developed a well thought out marketing strategy.

But You Won't Make This Mistake.

The ability to become a great marketer and do the activities that are necessary to attract and sell to the largest percentage of the best people who are perfectly suited for whatever you sell is within your reach! This book shows you how. The tips, tricks, and little known marketing techniques you're about to see as you flip through these pages have been proven to generate many tens of millions of dollars for my small businesses and for many others. In fact, these rare and unusual methods are making a fortune for many other people right now — and they can make a fortune for you, too. Use these methods and gain a genuine unfair advantage over all of your competitors!

And finally...

Working on your business is a lot like getting in top physical shape... It takes constant activity and great discipline to work yourself into shape and stay fit. You can't just go to the gym when you feel like it. So do spend at least one hour a day in concentrated thought of all the ways to build your business. That's 365 focused hours of <u>nothing</u> but thinking and dreaming creatively! One hour a day of doing <u>nothing</u> but focusing on how to build your business will help you dominate your market and destroy your competition! That's over two extremely productive weeks a year of <u>nothing</u> but planning — plotting — and scheming!

So with all that said, let's start dreaming and scheming together...

Direct-Response Marketing is a personal medium:

- Write and speak <u>to</u> <u>only</u> <u>one</u> <u>person</u>.

- The art is to make the person you are communicating with seem special.

- The more you can make them feel you are <u>only</u> <u>speaking</u> <u>to</u> <u>them</u> — the better.

W.I.F.M.

Strive to answer the question:

"What's in it for me?"

Use <u>plain</u> —
<u>direct</u> — <u>simple</u> —
and FORCEFUL
writing that goes
<u>straight</u> to the
emotions of
your reader.

Work ON it — not IN it.

Be the architect of your business — <u>not</u> the worker or foreman. Definition: The architect designs the building — and sees to it that his plans are followed by the builders. The same is true in business. We must design successful marketing systems — and then monitor them closely.

There are only 3 ways to build a business:

1. Get more customers.

2. Sell more high-ticket items — for bigger profits.

3. Sell more often to your customers!

> **Almost all million-dollar marketing ideas are transferable from one business to another.**

ೞೞ

Think in concepts.

See what others can't
see — or overlook.

ೞೞ

Emergency money-making generator...

When times get hard...

When business gets slow...

When you need cash-flow to feed the monster...

<u>All</u> <u>you</u> <u>do</u> <u>is</u>:

   a. Go to your best customers...

   b. Make them an irresistible offer they can't refuse!

   c. Have a special sale that will blow them away!

Do this and they'll stand in line with money in hand!

MASTERY

You do not become a MASTER by learning how to do 4,000 things... You become a MASTER by doing 12 important things 4,000 times!

We use hype and powerful promises for one reason:

<u>To</u> <u>cut</u> <u>through</u> <u>the</u> <u>clutter</u> of the thousands of advertising messages that are begging for our prospects and customers attention every single day.

◈ People are tuned out.

◈ They have created a tremendous resistance against ALL sales pitches.

◈ You have to do something dramatic to wake them up!

◈ You have to break through their zombie-like fog before you can pitch them.

The only way to do this is to be as dramatic as possible.

The best ideas are always an expansion and combination of previous ideas that worked.

Think on paper!

The very act of putting your ideas on paper forces you to think!

Your intimate understanding of your market and core business is the #1 ingredient for riches.

The more you know about the customer...

a. What they have bought before — or are buying now.

b. Their problems, frustration, pain, hopes, and dreams.

c. And how your product — service — company can offer them a solution to "B" — the more effective you can be at selling them.

Knowing MORE about your customer lets you MAXIMIZE the up-sell.

5 Elements Of Every Super-Successful Direct-Response Message:

1. Meaningful specifics — <u>not</u> vague generalities.

2. A promise.

3. An offer or offers.

4. Precise commands — *"Here's what I want you to do now."*

5. An extra reason to act immediately.

— Dan Kennedy

$ $ $ $ $

Customers in all markets want someone to do <u>everything</u> for them.

$ $ $ $ $

You must sell people the things they want — <u>NOT</u> the things you want to sell them!

* It's all about them, not you.

$ $ $ $ $

"Good Marketing Is A Combination Of Fishing And Chess!"

Eric Bechtold

All great fishermen know that the true secret to catching the big ones is:

1. Use the right bait.

2. Think like the fish!

3. <u>Never</u> reveal the hook.

All fishermen for sales and profits should pay attention!!

Focus on your strengths and make sure you have enough reliable people and systems in place to cover your weaknesses.

❖ ❖ ❖

Blur the lines between your work and play.

❖ ❖ ❖

OPERATION MONEY SUCK:

Invest <u>all</u> of your time, energy, and focus on all the various ways and means of sucking the maximum amount of moncy from your market.

99% of the focus should be on increasing your sales and profits. This is the life-blood of your business.

No business ever went under for having too many sales and profits!

STOP wasting your precious time, money, and energy on deadbeat prospects.

1. Do all you can to attract the very best prospects from all the rest.

2. As a general rule, those who have <u>recently</u> spent the most money or who re-buy from you on a regular basis are your <u>very</u> best prospects.

3. Develop new products and services that are as closely matched as possible to what they already bought from you.

4. Try to move your larger prospect group up the ladder — while spending the majority of your time and money on the smaller group of the highest qualified prospects.

5. Think of your entire base of customers and prospects as a triangle with the smaller group of the best buyers at the small tip on top. Can you see it? Good! Go ahead and draw it out. Then think about this: Your #1 strategy is to do all you can to increase the size and quality of the people at the top.

The **names** and **addresses**
of your best customers and their
past buying information can be
worth it's weight in diamonds!

*If you know what to do
with this list!*

♥ ♥ ♥ ♥ ♥

Selling is like the ritual of dating — the more you need them — the faster they run.

You must let them come to you. The prospect or customer must "feel" that they need you more than you need them.

♥ ♥ ♥

WAY

The average business person spends their day *"putting out brush fires"*... Their time and energy gets zapped by all the minor problems that come up from day to day. They are <u>never</u> able to pull back and work on their businesses.

There is no real game plan or strategy!

Many people think they are running their companies — but all they are doing is running the day-to-day operations...

They are locked into survival.

How to write a powerful hard-hitting sales letter:

1. Start with a big promise.

2. Paint the picture.

3. Give them proof.

4. Tell them <u>why</u> it's unique.

5. Close your argument by telling them why they must act now!

6. Make them a very special offer <u>if</u> they respond now!

7. End with a reminder of the promise — summary of offer — and STRONG call for action!

That's it! This is the blueprint or schematic of a sales letter — from start to finish.

❧Creativity☙

The creative process is <u>not</u> neat, clean, or pretty. It is not organized. It is dirty, messy, disorganized, and chaotic! It is filled with taking all kinds of unrelated ideas — and <u>mixing</u> <u>them</u> together in a very special way. It is deciding to do something — <u>without</u> knowing how you are going to do it. And then figuring it out as you go!

Roll-Out To Mega Wealth!

The same strategy that generated $1,000.00 can be rolled-out to generate $100,000.00 **if** the market is big enough — and other factors can be closely matched.

☞ THE HAND ☜

Every offer or promotion must meet these five crucial steps:

1. Is it the right offer?

2. Is it going to the right person?

3. Through the right media?

4. With the right hook?

5. And does it fit together with some kind of long-term plan?

There are only a handful — but they're vital. This lets you focus on the essentials.

(I borrowed this hand concept from *Bill Graham*, the greatest rock-n-roll promoter who ever lived! Bill had his 'handful' of ideas he used for every major event. This let him do BIG THINGS and make quick decisions. It will do the same for you, too!)

Great Quotes:

"People are silently begging to be led."

— Jay Abraham

"You can learn more from movement than meditation."

— Gary Halbert

"It doesn't have to be good — just good enough."

— Dan Kennedy

"All it takes is just one idea to make a million dollars!"

— Russ von Hoelscher

"We sell to creatures of emotion — bristling with prejudice — and motivated by pride and vanity."

— Dale Carnegie

◆ ◆ ◆

There is *so much joy* that comes
from the long-term effects of
a life of <u>hard work</u>, <u>discipline</u>,
<u>focus</u>, <u>goal setting</u>, <u>commitment</u>,
and <u>daily striving to work
towards your dream</u>.

Great Marketers
Are Hunters.

We are happiest when we're on the hunt. The bigger the hunt — the happier we are. *We must be reaching all the time.* All is well as long as our reach exceeds our grasp.

Build "risk reversal" into every offer.

★ Risk Reversal is taking all the pressure away from the prospect or customer...

★ It's an irresistible guarantee.

★ It's a dramatic promise that they must gain a major benefit — or they not only get their money back — but they will also receive something of tremendous value!

This blows them away — and will get you a lot of attention and interest.

Every prospect we seek is running around with a big sign around their neck that is flashing this message:

"Please make me feel important! And good about myself!"

However, only those with trained eyes can see this sign.

Fulfill the strong desire people have to feel...

- Important
- Esteemed
- Admired
- Beloved
- Special
- Observed

And they will give you everything they have!

❖ ❖ ❖

Direct Mail Marketing is really "Stealth Marketing." *You are flying under the radar!*

None of your competitors ever really know exactly what you're doing!
This is a smarter way to do business.

❖ ❖ ❖

The secret of lead generation: You are now a welcomed guest — not an annoying pest!

They sought you out. They are the ones who came to you! You did not go to them!

This difference in positioning is everything. It makes them interested, open, and responsive to your sales message.

Remember, people like to buy — but they hate being sold. Using lead generation makes them feel in control.

Look for things that are <u>HOT!</u>

"Whatever is current creates currency."

STEP ONE:

Find people to
sell shit to.

STEP TWO:

Find shit to sell
to those people!

Marketing is simply a 3-step process:

1. Attracting qualified leads.

2. Converting the highest percentage possible into first-time sales.

3. Re-selling the largest number of customers, as many times as you can, for the highest profit from each sale.

◆

These are the only 3 steps! However, each one must be done the right way.

The best ideas come to you in the heat of the moment!

Write down your best ideas when they are new — and when you are first getting started and very excited!

- These <u>ideas</u> <u>are</u> <u>HOT</u>! You'll need them later on when you are cold!!!

- Ideas are like slippery fish! Hard to hold onto! So you must capture them fast!

❧Cold Calling Sucks!☙

Build a marketing system that automatically brings you qualified prospects that have expressed a great interest and are very likely to buy.

It is <u>not</u> the job of your sales rep to cold-call and develop their own prospects.

2-Step Marketing is the safest and most profitable way to make money.

STEP ONE: Attract a highly qualified prospect.

- Use a great offer.
- Don't try to sell them too much at first.
- Get your hooks into them.
- Make it as easy as possible for them to buy the first time.
- Sell a low-priced widget.
- Educate them.
- Make them feel that *"They came to you"* — and <u>not</u> the other way around.

STEP TWO: SLAM THEM!

- Now bring out the BIG GUNS!
- You already have their attention and interest... Now you are in the position to show them how you can give them what they desire.

4 stages of learning anything new:

1. **<u>Unconscious</u> <u>Incompetence</u>:** You don't know what you don't know! Total Ignorance!

2. **<u>Conscious</u> <u>Incompetence</u>:** You begin to realize and discover the things you don't know. This is the frustration and confusion period. You're *still* incompetent... But, at least your eyes are beginning to open.

3. **<u>Conscious</u> <u>Competence</u>:** You can function in the new area — but, it's a major struggle — and you're not very good.

4. **<u>Unconscious</u> <u>Competence</u>:** MASTERY! You have mastered the main areas and you do it naturally — like a duck in the water!

Three Proven Ways To Make Money:

1. Do something nobody wants to do.

2. Do stuff others cannot be bothered to do — or would rather not do.

3. Do something you're great at that others are terrible at!!

—⦿⦿⦿—

Business is a combination of:

Art: We paint the canvas.

War: Battle the forces!

Science: Specific tested formulas.

Sport: Play the game!

Spiritual: Disciplined. Focused.

—⦿⦿⦿—

The Relationship Model:

1. Think customers — not sales.

2. Build relationships.

3. Spend money consistently to communicate with your customers.

4. Somehow we must convince them that...

- *We care.*

- *We want to help.*

- *We want to serve.*

- *And do <u>more</u> for them than any competitor.*

Most business owners have <u>no</u> systematic marketing strategy for getting and keeping customers.

They do everything they can think of — and some of what they're doing is working... But most have <u>never</u> thought deeply about the processes — and methods for:

1. Attracting new customers.

2. Selling them for the largest profit.

3. And then re-selling them as often as possible — for the <u>maximum</u> profits.

All of their marketing activities are hit and miss... They never quantify what is working the best. And, without this quantification — they can never combine the best methods into any kind of reliable automatic marketing system.

People are looking for and willing to spend a ton of money for:

<u>The</u> <u>Magic</u> <u>Pill</u>!

This is the product or service that they perceive can instantly and automatically give them something they badly want.

The power of the U.S.P.

(Unique Selling Position)

How can you separate yourself from every other competitor, in the most important way, to your average customer/prospect?

Answer that question in a clear and dramatic way — **AND GET RICH!**

<u>Stories</u> <u>Sell</u>!

You must create powerful stories
that captivate your prospects
and customers. These are stories
about you, your company, or
your products or services.

Choose your stories carefully. They
must sound real. They have to be
believable and emotional. *There
should be some drama!* Some special
secret — or a perceived benefit or
promise to the reader.

Stories help you make the sale
<u>when</u> <u>nothing</u> <u>else</u> <u>will</u>.

❖ ❖ ❖

Ruthless marketing has nothing to do with ripping people off. In fact, it's just the opposite.

It's all about extracting the largest amount of sales and profits from your targeted marketplace... And to do this — you must re-sell to the largest number of customers.

However, all ruthless marketers are relentless. You must develop the heart of the lion and the mind of the fox! You must be bold and audacious — and a bit cunning in order to seize the greatest opportunities for sales and profits.

It's not about lying to people or cheating them — but it is about mastering the art of getting the largest number of people in your market to give you the largest amount of their disposable income!

Spend one hour a day in concentrated thought of all the ways to build your business.

✓ That's 365 focused hours of <u>nothing</u> but thinking and dreaming creatively!

✓ One hour a day of doing <u>nothing</u> but focusing on how to build your business will help you dominate your market and destroy your competition!

✓ That's over 2 extremely productive weeks a year of <u>nothing</u> but planning — plotting — and scheming!

More Confidence = More Wealth!

From the book *Pour Your Heart Into It*:

"As I proved myself, my confidence grew. Selling, I discovered has a lot to do with self-esteem."

— Howard Schultz
CEO of Starbucks

<u>Howard</u> <u>is</u> <u>right</u>! The harder you work on building yourself — the more money you can make!

A Formula For Creating An Irresistible Offer:

1. Pile high and deeper!

   - *"You'll get this and this and this! And we'll also throw in this, if you act now!"*

   - <u>LOAD</u> <u>IT</u> <u>UP</u>!

   - Offer them a massive amount of stuff for their money!

2. STRONG REASON WHY.

   - There must be a strong reason <u>why</u> you are making them such a powerful offer.

   - The more believable the reason — the more they will respond.

3. Firm Deadline — with a powerful reason why.

   - <u>Everyone</u> <u>has</u> <u>deadlines</u>. The prospect doesn't believe them anymore. You must have a strong reason <u>why</u> the deadline is real.

4. A nice hook.

   - If you're going to create an irresistible offer — <u>it</u> <u>must</u> <u>really</u> <u>be</u> <u>irresistible</u>!

   - The "hook" is the foundation of <u>every</u> <u>offer</u>. It's got to sound really good — or they won't bite.

The key to massive productivity:

<u>Set</u> <u>higher</u> <u>goals</u>!

Commitments, deadlines, responsibilities, and pressures can be your best friend. They force you to do and be more.

###

Keep the pressure on:

###

In the midnight hour — when the deadlines are closing in — you are <u>forced</u> to make decisions.

- The walls of indecision begin breaking down.

- And the answers, which were once very muddy, now become clear.

Always begin with the end in mind.

You work backwards...

First, know what you want to accomplish.

Then decide your starting point — and move forward.

You figure it out, shape it, and fine-tune it as you go!

A good direct mail offer is nothing more than <u>a</u> <u>salesman</u> <u>in</u> <u>an</u> <u>envelope</u>.

The really cool thing is:

You can have thousands of these little salesmen working for you every single day!

Enthusiasm Sells!

If you're excited about what you do — it will attract others... People will gather around to watch you burn!

Enthusiasm makes up for all kinds of defects! After all, everyone loves a truly enthusiastic person.

$ $ $ $ $

To be a super-salesperson you have to believe strongly in whatever you are selling.

Selling is a transference of emotion! You must be sold <u>before</u> you can sell!

A great salesperson cannot make anyone buy something they don't want... That's why we must get prospects to "raise their hand" and show us that they are interested.

✓ Let the prospects qualify themselves by jumping through the hoops we hold in front of them!

✓ This is the secret to making easy sales!

❧Fail forward!❧

Q. What's the secret of success?

A. Making great decisions.

Q. What's the secret to making great decisions?

A. Make as many bad decisions as you can — as quickly as you can — and learn from them!

Wealth-Builder's Rule #1:

Make damn sure that the bulk of your income is not dependent on the number of actual hours you work. *After all, who makes more money — the brain surgeon or the rock star?*

The "4-M's" to create your own money-machine:

MODELS — Why create, when you can steal? What works for one will work for you. There are plenty of proven models you can steal from. Do it!

MARKETING — Attracting prospects and customers! Selling, re-selling, and re-selling again and again!

MARGINS — Make your promotions fail-proof... even with low response rates! Make your margins high! Higher! Highest!

MANAGEMENT — Organizing, systematizing, controlling, auto-pilot, absentee ownership mentality.

? ? ? ? ?

Why Direct Mail?

✓ Direct mail can give you tremendous leverage.

✓ Every direct marketing piece is a salesman in an envelope!

✓ It's out there working for you — and making huge numbers of sales, without your direct effort!

✓ Sending out 1,000 direct mail letters is like sending out a sales force of 1,000 of the best salespeople!

The power of take-away selling:

✓ <u>Nothing bothers people more than giving them something they really want — and then threatening to take it away</u>!

✓ The more they want it — and the more they <u>know</u> you can take it away — the more sales and profits you will make!

❧

Great marketers
see opportunities
where others cannot.

❧ ❧ ❧

If you <u>only</u> knew just how apathetic people are when they read your sales material you'd be shocked!

There are exceptions — but most people don't care! They have a great deal of unconscious (or even conscious) resistance <u>against</u> what you are saying.

You <u>must</u> be totally aware of this — <u>before</u> you can develop the correct strategies to deal with it.

The power of the 5 A.M. Club:

Force yourself to get out of bed before you want to — and put on a big pot of strong black coffee. — Pull out some paper and pens and start writing!

Ideas <u>will</u> come to you and through you — that you would <u>never</u> have discovered <u>if</u> you stayed in bed!

There is a magic at work here that's hard to explain! You must experience it — <u>before</u> you can believe it!

Wisdom from a Master Showman:

"It's not the audience who has the power — it's me! It is my talent and ability to know how to keep giving them what they want. I am in control — not them."

— Johnny Carson

This is a paradox:

YES, the market comes first. But it's your ability to "read" the market to discover the most powerful and profitable ways to serve it that counts.

The power is in your hands, not theirs.

Creativity comes from the labor of a driven and highly determined person!

Rebelliousness is also a key factor to creativity.

- Think outside the norm of your industry.

- Question everything.

- Be an independent thinker.

- Strive to be different!

Conformity breeds people who are as creative as a head of cabbage!

WE MUST BUY EVERY SALE WE MAKE!!!

We are in the business of buying sales at a profit!

We must constantly spend our money in proven ways that allow us to buy these sales at a profit.

Every new customer must be won! We must do something <u>BOLD</u> to attract them to us.

QUANTITY LEADS TO QUALITY.

The secret to coming up with the greatest ideas is to come up with lots of ideas! Go wild! Don't hold back! Just get into the habit of letting it flow! Set a time every morning for brainstorming as many ideas as you can come up with, make it fun and enjoyable to crank out huge quantities of ideas — *and you'll be amazed at the little gems that come out of this process!*

The art of being wise is the art of knowing what to overlook.

Fight for focus!

Spend the majority of your time on the few projects that can bring you the largest amount of sales and profits.

Ignore the advice from those around you who do not understand the big picture!

Prioritize!

T here's a lot of competition for your customers' money. <u>Never forget</u> <u>this</u>. If you can't answer the question: "Why should I give it to *you* and not *your competitor*?" then you don't deserve to be in business.

Just like in sports; the team who wants it more than the other team — wins!

You can <u>never</u> know the true value of something until and unless you compare it with something else.

◆

This is a powerful marketing strategy that you <u>must</u> incorporate into <u>all</u> of your sales material. Find as many ways as possible to associate yourself, your company, and your products and services with other items that have the greatest value in the minds and hearts of the people in your market.

❖ ❖ ❖

Stay very close
to your customer.

Know your customers <u>better</u> than
they know themselves. How? By
thinking about them all the time and
realizing that <u>the</u> <u>real</u> <u>reasons</u> they
buy are mostly unconscious.

❖ ❖ ❖

$ $ $ $ $

You must be a BIG THINKER to make BIG MONEY!

✓ First comes the GOAL (the mission, the focus, the target).

✓ Then come the specific strategies you will use to achieve this outcome.

✓ The why to do something is far more important than the how to do something.

✓ Work backwards. Establish the goals and the game plan first — then develop the steps to getting there.

$ $ $ $ $

⋈⋈⋈

Business is an amplified lifestyle.

It's life amplified! We deal with <u>more</u> problems, challenges, highs and lows, good times, bad times, headaches and hassles, joys and sorrows <u>in one year</u> than most people live with in an entire lifetime.

⋈⋈⋈⋈⋈

Business levels the playing field. Anyone with a strong desire to get rich and the willingness to do whatever it takes — CAN GET RICH!

Ideas are slippery fish!

They come in sudden flashes!
Write them down — <u>fast</u>!

The greatest entrepreneurs tend to be the worst managers. The skills it takes to build a business are usually the opposite of the skills it takes to manage it.

✿

The best stories to use in your sales material are **before-and-after stories**.

This is a powerful sales formula. The story tells about the problem and then it introduces the solution. Next it shows the great life-changing benefit. *The reader puts himself into the story and is sold!*

❈

It's always good to have more projects than you can comfortably handle.

❈ ❈ ❈

❖ ❖ ❖

The real business is between our ears and in our hearts — *not in the office!*

❖ ❖ ❖

I read a book on survival and it said that the #1 trait of successful survivalists is flexibility. So it is in business. The flexible person bends and adapts. The rest break.

Being flexible is all about:
changing, growing, adapting,
and moving forward.

Spend more money to make more money:

✓ "In direct marketing <u>it's the cost to get the sale</u> — not to make a mailing (or series of mailings) that counts." — *Jon Goldman*

✓ Many times, the secret is to spend more money, <u>not less</u>. This is especially true when you are making offers to your best prospects and customers.

**Human beings love to repeat
the same behaviors over
and over again.**

**If you can get them to do something
one time — you can get them to
do it the next time.**

⊙⊙⊙⊙⊙

The secret of a good direct mail letter:

It doesn't shout at people — it lures them in.

⊙⊙⊙

Working without a strong model is like...

taking a trip without a map.

True power is knowing your strengths and weaknesses.

Don't lie to yourself about these two areas. Most people tend to overestimate their chances of success and underestimate their chances of failure. You must become stronger in the areas you are already strong in and delegate (not abdicate) your weakest areas.

Find good people — and stay loyal to them:

It's always easier to maintain a relationship you already have — than to go out and start a new one.

The insiders are usually blind. Only an outsider can objectively look at something in a fresh, new way.

The <u>easiest thing</u> someone can do is stand on the sidelines and argue for the safe and conservative plan.

❖

It takes a hell of a lot courage to
step out and try new things,
but this is the only way to build
our businesses. *We must be bold!*

Header contains the "WAY NUMBER 88" stylized graphic.

WAY
NUMBER
88

Every once
in a while
you should ask
yourself:

⊠

"Do I own
a business
or a job?"

WAY

Wisdom from the notorious
takeover artist,
T. Boone Pickens:

"Business is not life. Life is tragic. Business is fun! It's like a game you play. It's more like playing a game of racquetball than living life."

**We are all self-made...
but only the successful
will admit it.**

When you say, "YES!" to one thing and totally put your heart into it — you are automatically saying "No!" to many other things.

✳ ✳ ✳

The adversities in life can make us stronger… and that's great, because business is a constant adversity.

✳ ✳ ✳

∽MOST∽
self-employed people have a terrible boss!

The only **real power** you have over other people is the power to **influence** or **persuade them**.

You can make
more money with
1% of 100
peoples' efforts —
*than with 100%
of your own
individual efforts.*

The 4 laws of self teaching:

1. *You are your greatest teacher.*

2. You can learn <u>anything</u> you want to learn.

3. You <u>must</u> take total responsibility for everything that happens to you.

4. Experience + Reflection = Wisdom!

❦

Step out in faith — and figure it out *as you go!*

❦

The great Olympic runner,
Steve Prefontaine said:

"There may be men who can beat me — <u>but</u> <u>they'll</u> <u>have</u> <u>to</u> <u>bleed</u> <u>to</u> <u>do</u> <u>it</u>!"

Product knowledge is highly overrated.

Every salesperson is trained in extensive product knowledge. <u>FORGET THAT</u>! <u>Prospect</u> <u>knowledge</u> <u>is</u> <u>more</u> <u>important</u> <u>than</u> <u>product</u> <u>knowledge</u>. Prospects buy perceived benefits and results. They do not buy product information.

A successful business is constantly changing, developing, evolving, and growing! It's like a living organism that evolves to meet the demands of the environment.

People want to do business with people just like them.

"I have a lot of competition, but <u>ZERO</u> competitors!"

— *Kerry Thomas*

$ $ $

I LIKE DEBT...

Part of the fun is to have the constant pressure to meet your financial obligations.

The carrot and the stick are both great motivators... But the stick is more important!

$ $ $

If your back-end business is strong — you should set out to lose as much money as you possibly can to make the first sale to new customers.

Your first sale sets up all the future sales... The only purpose of your first sale is to build enough relationship with the new customer to get the next sale.

105

Nothing gives you
freedom like having
**a few bucks
in the bank!**

When asking,
ASK BOLDLY.

WAY
NUMBER
107

A person's greatest need is to feel appreciated...

You must make them feel important and special and needed — without appearing phony. This is very difficult. But the world's most successful people have mastered this powerful skill.

The 12 Paths to Power:

1. **Know yourself intimately.** People tend to overestimate their chances of success and underestimate their chances of failure. What do you really want? What are your strengths and weaknesses? What are you best at?

2. **Be an information filter and a knowledge sponge.** Keep searching for the truth! Keep trying to figure out other people and WHY they do what they do. Greater knowledge of yourself and the world gives you a wider range of possible actions to choose from.

3. **Get it together.** FOCUS. Focus on what you want. Most people want it all, and they aren't very powerful.

4. **Live an upright life.** Honesty is the best policy.

5. **Take a shot.** If you don't play, you won't win. GO FOR IT! MASSIVE ACTION.

6. **Hang in there.** "Persevere, no matter the pain, persevere." — *H. Ross Perot*

7. **Pick do-able objectives.** Pick battles you can win! Don't waste your time and energy fighting losing battles.

8. **Don't make a big deal about being the boss.** Be humble. You need other people to help you win.

9. **Don't motivate other people to oppose you.** Don't make people any more jealous than they already are! Don't strip someone down and cause them to seek revenge.

10. **Put your adversities to good use.** Adversity can contain the energy you need to succeed.

11. **Calm down.** Open-ended desires lead to nothing. Be satisfied with what you have, AND THEN, keep pushing! Relax and enjoy!

12. **THINK WIN/WIN.** Empower yourself and help others get what they want.

The power of simplicity:

If you can't sum up your basic offer in one sentence — go back to the drawing board.

All marketing
lies in <u>two</u> <u>words</u>:

attraction and retention.

Do everything possible to shift the power and get them to chase you — *rather than you chasing them!*

Are you a professional or an amateur?

The difference: Amateurs only work hard when they feel like it. Professionals work just as hard whether they feel like it or not.

"Marketing is simply
a combination of math
and psychology."

— *Dan Kennedy*

Our job as marketers is to *attract* the right people and *repel* the wrong ones.

What do all people want? Someone to do it for them! That's why all of us should be in the "do-it-for-em" business!

**All this talk about retirement
is nonsense! Work gives our lives
purpose, meaning, and structure.
Stop telling me to take it easy...**
I'll have eternity to take it easy!

><del></del>•<del></del><

In business, if you rest, you rust.

WAY
NUMBER
118

• • • • • • • • • • • • • • • •

**Does talent create its own opportunities?
Or does your total passion and commitment to
the opportunities create its own talent?**

• • • • • • • • • • • • • • • • •

**Neatness rejects
involvement.
Dumb your sales
letters down.
*Make them
look homely.***

❧❧❧

Key to great
sales material:

Write lots of copy
and edit it down.

❧❧❧

Playing it safe is <u>no guarantee</u> against misfortune.

The way to sell the *unfamiliar* is to link it with the *familiar*.

❖ ❖ ❖

**It's far better to have a friendship
that is centered around the business
— than to have a business that's
centered around a friendship.**

*Business is at its <u>best</u> when it is
honestly selfish.* Strive to keep it
that way with all your relationships.

❖ ❖ ❖

WAY
124

Jump — and the net will appear!

✓ Make the commitment first.

✓ Set the deadline!

✓ Run the ad — then scramble to put the fulfillment together!

✓ Make <u>BIG</u> <u>PROMISES</u> to groups of customers — and then scramble to make them real!

✓ Do whatever you can to force yourself to do more!

The question all marketers
<u>must</u> constantly ask:

What's next?

$ $ $

Happiness is...
a never-ending stream of positive cash-flow!

$ $ $

You must create "Exclusivity."

There <u>must</u> be something that automatically separates you — your company — and the stuff you sell — from all the other competitors.

This "something different" <u>must</u> be very important to your customers — and must be created by you.

Salespeople get paid to hear the word "no!"

▨ ▨ ▨

A "no" does not mean "no" to the aggressive person who wants the sale!

"When people are free to do as they please, they usually imitate each other."

— *Eric Hoffer*

•••••••••••◎◎◎◎◎•••••••••••

Retirement = Death.

•••••••••••◎◎◎◎◎•••••••••••

Constantly look for things that are <u>hot</u> <u>now</u>! Feed the existing hunger in the marketplace! Look for ways to put a new twist on things that are making huge sums of money right now.

"Find a parade and get in front of it."

— *John Carlton*

Residual income is the life-blood of your business.

You <u>must</u> put some consistent thought and action into all the ways and means — to get this type of income flowing through your company.

WAY
NUMBER
133

Better to **strengthen your back** than to lighten your load!

✿ ✿ ✿

WAY
NUMBER
134

Strive to become the
competitor you would hate
to compete against!

Knowing <u>what</u> to do will always make you more money than knowing <u>how</u> to do it.

You can figure out all the details later — or better yet — let someone else figure them out.

The secret to making <u>more</u> <u>money</u> in your business can be summed up in two words:

☞ THINK BIGGER! ☜

✓ You gotta keep your eye on the multi-million dollar (or billion!) prize!

✓ You <u>must</u> be willing to walk over a lot of $100.00 bills to get to the millions or billions you want.

✓ In other words, it's a fight for FOCUS! You must constantly put all of your time, attention, energy, and resources on the areas that can make you the most money.

The heart rules the mind!
(That's why we <u>must</u>
sell to their emotions!)

In any negotiation...

The person who pretends like they need or want it <u>the</u> <u>least</u> — WINS!

Let your communications buzz with excitement!

The <u>greatest sin of all</u> is to bore somebody!

The value of an employee is determined by 2 things:

1. How much money they <u>directly</u> bring into the company? (In other words, without their <u>direct</u> effort — this money would not have come in.)

2. How difficult will they be to replace?

Nothing else matters.

◆ ◆ ◆

The right stories will easily warm people up and prepare them for the close.

◆ ◆ ◆

❧❧❧

"You must enter the conversation that's already in their mind."

— *Robert Collier*

Every great story has
two essential elements:
TENSION & DISCOVERY.

It's all about pressure and
release! Build the pressure,
create the tension, make it real,
and then introduce the discovery!
Now you can sell them!

An entrepreneurial rule for choosing new ventures:

In any new business venture
— if it's not a stretch —
don't do it! It must scare
you and induce some risk.
<u>If not, don't do it</u>.

ಶಿ ಶಿ ಶಿ ಶಿ ಶಿ

Take good care of the people who take good care of you!

ಶಿ ಶಿ ಶಿ

**Put your entire focus on
making a BIGGER PIE —
not on counting and
weighing each slice!**

**All growth comes from
consciously living outside
of your comfort zone.**

❦

**If you're not doing things
on a regular basis that scare you
just a little (or a lot!)
— you're not growing.**

WAY
NUMBER
148

> **Everybody loves
> an offer they perceive
> is just for them.**
>
> **The things they want
> the most are the things
> others cannot get!**

Success is the ability to outrun failure!

"Business is a good game — lots of competition and a minimum of rules. You keep score with the money."

— Nolan Bushnell

❧❧

The Power of Focus...

Don't spend your time managing problems. Spend your time building your opportunities.

❧❧

The best marketing is <u>always</u> in a constant state of flux.

***Most people* are secretly
looking for someone to lead
them by the hand.**

You serve yourself
best — *when you serve
others the most.*

Your marketing (everything you do
to get more customers and keep
them spending more money for life)
is only limited by your imagination.

*Remember that every time
you are going through a sales slump
or a cash-flow crisis.*

**Keep feeding the fire of your enthusiasm —
so it <u>always</u> burns brightly!**

- ✓ Get involved in exciting new projects that stir your blood!

- ✓ Stay excited about the future!

- ✓ Set bigger goals and grander visions!

- ✓ "If you want to turn your hours into minutes, renew your enthusiasm!"
  Papyrus

You can't have
the glory...
IF YOU DON'T
HAVE THE GUTS!

People hate to be "sold" — but they love to "choose."

Spend <u>more</u> money — to close more sales!

1. You can't go wrong if you are spending this money on super qualified prospects.

2. You are selling big ticket items with good margins.

In some cases (as long as your percentage of conversion is going up) you can't spend too much money!

Keep searching for products and services with the largest gap between perceived value and actual cost.

These are the items that can make you rich!

Look for items where the prospect doesn't know or care about your actual cost.

WAY
161

◈

**Customers go where they
arc invited and stay where
they are appreciated.**

After a while, you **STOP** listening to what other people say — and *only* pay attention to what they do.

Think of the groups of leads you attract into your business as a HUGE TON of dirt, mud, and rocks — with a few solid gold nuggets mixed in with all this filth! Your job is to keep sifting through all the mud and crap to find these gold nuggets!

You must sift through this rubble in the cheapest possible way — so the majority of your marketing costs can be invested in the gold nugget group — not the muddy group!

Most marketers are weak.

They quit way too soon.

They are too worried about offending their prospects or customers.

Or, they simply don't know that there is a great deal more money laying on the table that could and should be theirs — if they simply went after it more aggressively and then stayed after it until they got it!

"The most important thing in life
is not to capitalize on your gains.
Any fool can do that! The really important
thing is to profit from your losses.
That requires intelligence and it
makes the difference between
a wise man and a fool."

William Boltho, Twelve Against the Gods

＊ ＊ ＊

Take away selling:

Sometimes when you say "No!" — it only makes them want you more!

＊ ＊ ＊

WAY
NUMBER
167

Continuing to make <u>BIG</u> <u>MONEY</u> over a period of years never happens by accident. It is *always* the result of high intention, sincere effort, intelligent direction, and skillful execution. It represents the wise choices of many alternatives and the cumulative experience you gain from all the years of disciplined and focused work.

"I've seen companies so obsessed with competition that they keep looking in their rearview mirror and crash into a tree."

— Sergey Brin
Co-Founder of Google.com

Create as many
"businesses within
your business" as
you possibly can.

Go out of your way to
show people that you are
<u>REAL</u> and vulnerable —
and they will emotionally
open up to you.

Love and hate play an important role in the creative process.

⚜ To begin a project — you must fall completely and totally in love with it! And while in love — write <u>all</u> of the promotional materials!

⚜ And to complete the project — you must <u>hate</u> <u>it</u> in the worst way and want nothing more than to be done with it so you can move on to something else!

good direct-response follow-up sequence works like the Chinese torture method where you are strapped to a table and a small drop of water hits your forehead every two seconds. After a while you go mad!

good follow-up campaign does the same thing: <u>It breaks down the sales resistance of your prospects</u>. After a while they say, "NO MORE! You've got me! Count me in — here's my money!"

Get your *best offer* in front of <u>more people</u> and follow-up like crazy!

ಎ ✿ ಲ

174

❧◆❧

The best product does not always win, *but the best marketing always does!*

ost people run their businesses like a person who drives with one foot on the gas pedal and the other foot on the brake pedal!

What a joke! A better analogy to run your business is the way champion race car drivers win their races: all of their attention and energy is focused on the road ahead. They only think of winning and their concentration is totally in the moment.

Damn the critics!

The critics of this world are little-thinkers who are controlled by their doubts and fears.

They love to pick a new idea apart — but often all they do is analyze it to death!

These people <u>think</u> they are being smart — but what they are really doing is thinking small. Their entire focus is on the difficulties rather than the possibilities.

The bottom line: <u>It's easier to criticize</u>. It's easier to think small and look for all the things that can go wrong. This type of thinking requires zero courage.

Great companies die because the BIG thinking action-oriented entrepreneurs who built them are replaced by "middle managers" who love to sit around and have meetings and discuss what they're going to talk about at the next meeting.

They see all the risks and do nothing.

Negative motivation often works <u>much</u> <u>better</u> than anything positive!

The stick is always better than the carrot!

WAY
178

◼ ◼ ◼

**The mass of men are usually
wrong about everything!**

*Do the opposite of what
everyone else does and you
will almost always succeed!*

◼ ◼

Every business deal is always much easier to get into than to get out of...

- ◈ Especially for those of us who are eternal optimists!

- ◈ So please try to think everything through as clearly as possible from all angles — while you are high on the idea.

- ◈ How does it fit with your BIGGER plan?

- ◈ What are the exit strategies?

- ◈ What happens if it doesn't work out?

- ◈ The answers to these questions can save you years of heartache.

Whoever said: "Do what you love and the money will follow" was wrong! It should be:

"<u>Learn</u> to love the activities that are capable of producing the largest sum of money — and the money will follow!"

Your business is like a bicycle. Either you keep it moving or you fall down!

★ Keep searching for your next big winner!

★ Keep finding better ways to give your customers and prospects what you know they want the most!

Use more premiums to drive your sales and profits! *Here's how:*

1. Choose or develop the ultimate premium of the greatest value to your market.

2. Sell the FREE premium! Make it the star of your show!

3. The only catch: The product or service comes along with your FREE premium on a trial basis.

4. Let them keep the premium if they return the item you are selling.

Great premiums work because:

a. They overcome the apathetic laziness and fear that most prospects feel when they see your pitch.

b. If you choose the right premium — they let you harness the power of greed!

<u>Objections are great!</u>

◈ Never run from objections. You can turn each one into a solid reason for buying!

◈ List every single possible objection. Then create a multi-page report called: "Your BIGGEST Questions Answered!" Each question is an objection. Your answer erases every possible doubt in their minds.

◆ ◆ ◆

Life, love, and business favor the bold!

◆ ◆ ◆

Revolution accelerates evolution!

Be bold and innovative!

Test your wildest ideas!

Experiment like crazy!

Radical change is the key to discovering new ideas that can make you rich! Keep your business in a state of constant flux. *Make "change" your #1 product.*

$ $ $ $ $

What you sell and what you "really" sell are two different things.

- "In our factory, we make lipstick. In our advertising, we sell hope." — *Charles Revlon*

- "Kodak sells film, but they don't advertise film. They advertise memories." — *Theodore Levitt*

- What you "really" sell is all that touch-feely emotional crap that you must connect to whatever gizmo you're pushing.

$ $ $ $ $

❖❖❖❖❖

Wise men have
<u>many</u> doubts.

❖❖❖❖❖

Stay very focused on your market
every day and you will be in the
market for many years! Your
market is your meal ticket for life!

The #1 reason that the most solid businesses begin to decline is simply because they <u>STOP</u> doing the things that took them to the top.

◆ They lose their edge.

◆ They lose their focus.

◆ They lose their hunger.

◆ They lose the boldnees and creativity they had when they were struggling their way to the top. They become conservative and complacent. Now they are easy targets for all of the others who are just like they once were!

Don't try to figure things out too quickly. **Let your ideas have time to ferment.**

▣ The best ideas for building your business are like all of the ingredients you put in the pot when you're making chili. Any good cook will tell you that the "secret" is not only adding the right ingredients — but letting it stew.

▣ Great ideas are like this, too.

▣ You must be willing to go through the pain of confusion. You <u>must</u> suffer through many twists and turns along the path — to get to your final destination. It's 3 steps forward and 2 steps back all along the way. You are constantly stumbling around in the dark looking for the light switch!

Because so many people these days are skeptical — and so many marketers are lying every time they open their mouths — <u>you</u> <u>can</u> <u>use</u> <u>brutal</u> <u>honesty</u> as your marketing weapon!

Tell them what to do — *but not how to do it!*

Here's a cute formula to summarize the steps we are all supposed to be focusing on to make the largest sum of money. It's a simple 4-step formula for maximizing profitability:

MEET • CONVERT • UPGRADE • EXPAND

MEET: Meet the right prospects. These are the people who are most likely to want what you have and give you the maximum amount of money for the longest period of time.

CONVERT: Convert the largest number of these people into first-time buyers. Make it as easy as possible to get them to do business with you the first time.

UPGRADE: Once you have them — focus on upgrading them. Make them your biggest and best offer! Try to separate the most serious from the rest. Get them while they're in heat and sell them as much as you can right away!

EXPAND: Then try to extend the relationship with these customers for as long as possible! Stay in close touch with them. Build a strong bond of friendship with them. Sell them as much stuff as you possibly can — for as long as you can! Strive to create a lifetime of never-ending revenue from all the repeat business you do with them!

REPEAT: Repeat the previous 4 steps in the biggest and boldest way!

General George Patton had one simple rule for warfare that works like magic in business. **Every battle plan must be carried out with 3 things:**

Speed!

Simplicity!

Boldness!

Your marketing plans must incorporate these 3 elements. Strike FAST, strike HARD, and strike OFTEN!

**Money may not
make you happy...
but it will help
calm your nerves!**

❋

**It's always better to
have it and not need it
than to need it
and not have it!**

"The gold is in your existing clients."

— Joe Polish

Business is a lot like that popular reality show on TV — "Survivor." The object of that game is to:

- Outwit

- Outlast, and

- Outplay your competition!

We __must__ do this, too!

No matter what you sell — there's always some part of it that you can give away for free.

By doing this — you make people feel like they owe you something in return. Now they are ready and willing to listen to what you have to say. And if you do it right — you will make them see the value of whatever you're selling and make them want to pay you the full price for it.

Offering them something for free wakes them up! It makes it super easy for serious prospects to raise their hand and say, "Okay, give it to me now!" It separates you from all the other competitors who *never* do this. And it gets you in the door and makes it so simple and easy to sell them!

People are much more *influenced* by the height of your enthusiasm than the depth of your knowledge.

All business is
show business!

❖ ❖ ❖ ❖ ❖

Love will find a way — indifference will find an excuse.

✓ Learn to love the things you do that bring you the largest number of sales and profits!

✓ Love makes all burdens light. This is the key to doing your <u>best</u> work!

❖ ❖ ❖ ❖ ❖

Your best customers are like fires. They go out if unattended.

The key word is "relationship."

The better they "feel" about you — the more money they will give you!

Remember, the fire never dies as long as you keep feeding it!

"What are you willing to do?"

❖

The answer to these six words will determine how much money you will ultimately make.

Catch yourself on fire and they will come to watch you burn!

Winston Churchill said it best:

❝Before you can inspire with emotion, you must be swamped with it yourself.❞

The 5-Step Problem/Solution Copywriting Formula for making prospects want whatever you sell:

Step One: First tell them what they could be getting or how things could be.

Paint a bright picture!

Step Two: Then introduce the problem by telling them what they are getting now.

You are searching for people in pain. the more specific you can be about their main problems, the more they will feel that you are speaking directly to them.

Step Three: Now introduce your product or service as the ultimate solution!

Now you have their full interest!

Step Four: Now back-up as many of your claims as you can. Everyone who reads every word you write is skeptical. In other words, they don't believe a word you say!

Step Five: Then summarize all four steps a couple of times in a couple of different ways.

Dumb it down and hit on your main selling points from the previous four steps.

Try this formula, it works! You expand the need for what you offer and make people want to buy it now!

Many business people who pride themselves greatly for being very conservative in the way they carefully think everything through — are not conservative at all. <u>They're</u> <u>scared</u>!

- They think they're being careful, but what they are really doing is being totally controlled by fear and limited thinking.

- For every wild-eyed big-thinking entrepreneur who blows up their company because of their reckless actions — there are probably 100,000 business people who are playing it *way too safe* and losing out on all kinds of money that could and should be theirs.

The marketers' <u>most</u> <u>important</u> <u>asset</u> is his or her knack for putting themselves in the position of their customers and for addressing *their* most important needs.

There is no beginning, middle, and end to the creative process.

Your best ideas will evolve as you move forward!

Each new idea can be the seed for many new ideas.

Your <u>best</u> <u>work</u> is *always* still out there!

Your personal stories are <u>the</u> <u>best</u> <u>way</u> to drive home your strongest selling messages.

◈ Your stories contain emotional power!

◈ They bypass the prospect's brain and go right to the heart!

◈ Your best prospects will not only remember your main stories, they will be able to repeat them back to you in exact detail!

◈ Your best stories will become a strong bond that <u>will</u> connect you to your prospect!

◈ Your stories are 100% proprietary! They are yours and yours alone. *Only you are uniquely qualified to tell your stories.* This is your best way to separate yourself from your other competitors and gain a foothold into the minds and hearts of the people in your market.

"The road to excess leads to enlightenment!"

— William Blake
(A man who pushed the envelope!)

✓ You <u>never</u> know how far you can go until and unless you push yourself way too far!

✓ You push it hard — until it breaks — then fix it — then push it even harder, until it breaks again!

✓ Whoever said, "Don't bite off more than you can chew," was wrong! The secret to wealth is to constantly be involved in way more projects than you can possibly handle! You must boldly push beyond your limits in order to expand them. The higher you climb, the more you can see... SO KEEP CLIMBING HIGHER!

NEVER promote a product or service that you can't explain in 3 minutes!

▣ Or at least cover the major benefits!

▣ Does this sound impossible? It's not! Genius is the art of making complicated things "seem" simple.

WAY
NUMBER
212

> "As I proved myself,
> my confidence grew.
> Selling, I discovered has a lot
> to do with self-esteem."
>
> — *Howard Schultz,*
> *CEO of Starbucks*
>
> Howard is right! The harder you work on
> building yourself — the more money you
> can make!

Make your sales material *outrageous!*

› Do <u>not</u> be afraid to make it bigger and bolder!

› Make it louder!

› Make it somewhat controversial.

› Too much of the sales material I see is neat, clean, pretty, carefully written, and boring as hell! You must dare to be different! WAKE THEM UP! Don't be afraid of offending people. In fact, you must offend the wrong people to attract the right ones!

WAY
NUMBER
214

Customers are and will always be totally self-centered. They don't care about you. Never have. Never will. They only care about what you can do for them — better, faster, and less expensively.

We all write "Dear Friend" when addressing our customers — but in reality, they are not our friends. *They are demanding tyrants who must be served!*

The true art of selling is to
make people feel that they are
the ones chasing you!

◆

To be very aggressive with your
marketing <u>without</u> appearing like
you need or even care whether
they do business with you.

Find the buyers who can buy the most and you won't have to find the most buyers!

Less is more!

If you <u>only</u> knew just how apathetic people are when they read your sales material you'd be shocked!

- There are exceptions — but most people don't care! They have a great deal of unconscious (or even conscious) resistance <u>against</u> what you are saying.

- You must be totally aware of this — <u>before</u> you can develop the correct strategies to deal with it.

WAY
218

�֍ �֍ �֍

Who are your real enemies?
They're <u>not</u> who you think!

Your real enemies are the people who tell you
what you want to hear and completely agree
with everything you do. They try to pump your
ego — pat you on the back — laugh at your
stupid jokes — and all the other "yes-men."

These people are your enemies because they will
lull you to sleep if you let them. They will pull
you down into the quicksand of smugness and
self-satisfaction. Because of this — you will
lose your edge.

What you need are people who will get in your
face and tell you that you are wrong! People
who challenge you and stimulate you into taking
new actions and striving to do and become more
than you are now!

✖ ✖ ✖

In good times and bad, there will *always* be a market for things that nobody needs!

If you want to eek out a comfortable living, sell things that people need.

If you want to get rich — sell things that people want!

• •

MONEY IS
LIKE MANURE...

You gotta spread it around and mix it up in some good soil and throw in the right seeds — otherwise it is worthless.

- If you pile it up and don't use it — it stinks!

- Keep spreading it around in as many things as possible that keep you excited and moving forward.

• •

Joe Karbo's famous headline reads: **"Most people are too busy making a living to get rich."** He couldn't have been more right!

The majority are prisoners of petty thinking. They go through life asking for so little. Their priorities are all screwed up!

There are so many forces against the ambitious person who wants to make many millions of dollars.

Blow your own horn!

Nobody's going to blow
your horn for you — you gotta
get out there and do it!

The "perception" that you always have something "new" and exciting to share with them is one of the things that will *always* keep them coming back for more!

* What messages can you send out to your market that keeps them eager to hear from you?

* How can you keep it "fresh" in the minds and hearts of your older and more established core customers who have already heard your story a million times?

Carlos Gambino, the powerful Mob boss, rose from the bottom to the top with this simple philosophy:

"Have the heart of the lion
and the mind of the fox."

Qualities of THE LION:

Powerful • Forceful • Strong • King of the Jungle •
Killer (but also playful) • Brave • Independent •
Agile • Fearless

Qualities of THE FOX:

Careful • Cunning • Smart • Invisible • Elusive •
Fast • Shrewd

The lion is the king of the jungle and
roars loudly! The fox is hard to spot and catch!
He is quick and smart.

*This simple philosophy not only
made Carlos Gambino the most powerful
Mob boss ever — but he
never spent a day of his life in jail!*

❦❧❦❧

Blur the lines between <u>work</u> and <u>play</u>.

Database marketing in 3 words:

★ **Segment**

★ **Concentrate**

★ **Dominate!**

WAY
NUMBER
227

Wisdom from rock-n-roll hall of famer, *Tom Petty (one of the most successful and prolific singer/songwriters in history):*

"Other people take vacations and go to Hawaii and play golf or scuba dive. This is what I do. I write songs and I make records."

Stay 100% focused on your work. Master it. Let it become the best part of who you are. Stay totally committed to becoming the <u>best</u> you can be. Fall in love with what you do! And always strive to become even better.

This is the closest thing to true happiness I have ever discovered.

Here is one of my favorite quotes
that is right next to my big clock,
so I can see it all the time:

**❝Business is <u>always</u> a struggle.
There are always obstacles and
competitors. There is never an open
road, except the wide road that
leads to failure. Every great
success has always been achieved
by fight. Every winner has scars.
Those who succeed are the efficient
few. They are the few who have the
ambition and willpower to develop
themselves.❞**

— Herbert N. Casson

Your goal for each day is to come up with <u>at least</u> <u>one</u> <u>new</u> <u>idea</u> that you *didn't* have yesterday for increasing your sales and profits!

**The golden key to burnout is to
fall back in love with your work.**

℘℘℘

What were the things that pumped you up
in the beginning? Why did you love them?
How can you fill your life with more of the
things that excited you the most?

The true secret of success is to be bold and tenacious!

Put it all out there. <u>Don't</u> hold back even for a single second. Express yourself fully — to the point of being totally outrageous! Mix this with a high degree of tenacity and you'll shoot straight to the top! Nothing can hold you back as long as you have these two qualities. You will leapfrog over all those cold and timid souls who <u>never</u> put their whole heart and soul into <u>anything</u> and then give up at the first sign of adversity.

"Give a man enough audacity and tenacity and he will surely rule the world."

— *Marcus Aurelius*

"Few things are impossible to diligence and skill."

— Samuel Johnson

◎ All super successful entrepreneurs are diligent people who have developed and mastered at least a few key skills that have taken them to the top.

◎ Hard work + persistence = diligence. It's not a word we use a lot these days, but we should. It means working your ass off — being totally driven — and not giving up until you achieve your objective.

◎ When you are diligent, nothing can stop you. If you can't go around it or over or under it, you'll charge right through it. And if at first you don't succeed, you will pick yourself back up again and keep fighting.

◎ Do this long enough and hard enough, and you will ultimately develop the skills you need.

◎ Developing the skills you need to make huge sums of money (or whatever else you want) can take a lot of time and effort. The ones who are most skilled are those who are driven to the point of obsession and have consistently paid the highest price.

◎ Everyone wants the result, but very few are willing to put in the time and intense effort to get it.

🔲 🔲 🔲 🔲 🔲

Never fear objections!

Bring 'em on!

🔲 🔲 🔲

"Most people would kill just
to be treated like a god for
only one brief moment."

— *Gene Hackman's character
from the movie "Hoosiers"*

The only **3** ways to make money:

1. <u>Sell your time for money</u>. You charge by the hour and trade your life for a paycheck.

2. <u>Sell a product or service</u>. Your money comes from the sale of the gizmo — not the time or work it takes to sell it.

3. <u>Passive income</u>. Your money makes you more money <u>without</u> your direct effort. All of the world's richest people make their money with the third method. Their money comes to them automatically from a wide variety of cash-producing investments. Their money keeps making them more money! Do everything you can to make as much of your money as possible in the third area! What would you rather be: A rock star or a brain surgeon?

◇ ◇ ◇ ◇ ◇

The best sales material is like fine wine — it needs time to age.

◈ My best sales promotions have one thing in common — they are jobs that took two or three weeks to do. I let my best ideas grow and take on a life of their own.

◈ I worked on them slowly and figured it all out as I went along. It took some time to do all of this — but the results speak for themselves. Of course, now you can always go back and re-write this letter over and over again! So what took you weeks can now be re-done in a matter of days or even hours!

◇ ◇ ◇ ◇ ◇

⤎⧸⧹⤏

"When you advertise fire extinguishers, open with the fire."

Advertising Legend,
— David Ogilvy

No matter how bad your business may be right now — as long as you have a huge list of customers — you are <u>always</u> only one irresistible offer away from making bazillions of dollars!

The 5 Main Reasons you should be developing and selling MORE informational products and services:

<u>Reason #1</u>: **Differentiation.** This is the ultimate way to separate yourself from all of the other people who are trying to get more money from your best prospects and customers.

<u>Reason #2</u>: **Huge profits!** The amount of money you can get people to gladly give you has very little or even <u>nothing</u> to do with your actual cost to produce it!

<u>Reason #3</u>: **The ultimate marketing magnet!** Everyone respects a published author. This is the greatest way to <u>wake</u> <u>the</u> <u>right</u> <u>people</u> <u>up</u>! You will make the right prospects, Joint Venture partners, and other influential people want to do business with you. It's the ultimate icebreaker! It's the most powerful way to let the <u>right</u> people get to know you and respect you.

<u>Reason #4</u>: **You get paid to develop your expertise!** To teach is to learn twice! Selling information is the greatest way to reach out and try to help people. However, you can never sincerely try to help someone else *without* helping yourself.

<u>Reason #5</u>: **This is a positive addiction with almost <u>no</u> side effects!** Developing and selling info products is addictive! It's such a RUSH to come up with a new idea and quickly turn it into massive profits! This is fun and rewarding! It's such a creative and fulfilling way to make huge sums of money!

There is no better time to sell information. This is the greatest solution to the major problem of aggressive competitors who are all fighting hard to get the same dollars you are trying to get. The costs to produce great information products is getting lower all the time... and the amount of choice you have to make GIANT PROFITS is only limited by your imagination.

Most people are penny wise and dollar foolish.

They're walking over the dollars to get to the dimes!

It's so insane, and yet I see this crazy behavior manifested in a multitude of ways.

These people lack vision. They just can't see the BIG PICTURE. They are totally controlled by their fear, greed, and stupidity.

The easy way to dramatically increase your persuasive power: <u>WRITE</u> <u>MORE</u>!

Consistent writing about your #1 subject helps to crystalize your thinking.

This, in turn, <u>will</u> make you a much more persuasive thinker. You will speak with greater confidence and power. Your ideas will be sharper and more people will want to buy and re-buy from you.

<u>Problems</u> and <u>pain</u>
ARE GOOD THINGS!

Competitive people see problems
and pain as challenges. *They use
the pressure of adversity to spur them
on to new heights!*

WAY
NUMBER
243

The 9 Major Marketing Mistakes
and How to Avoid Them!

1. **No Focus:** The list of prospects is #1. Hone in on one specific highly qualified prospect. Know them in the most intimate way.

2. **No Compelling Offer:** You must have something hot to get people to take action now!

3. **No Deadline:** The more urgency you can build into your offer — the higher your response rate will be!

4. **No Testimonials:** What other people say about you is much more important than what you say about yourself.

5. **No Measurement of Results:** The only thing that counts is ROI (Return on Investment). Know your numbers! Don't get hung up on response rates.

6. **No Follow-Up:** Most people are giving up on 'em way too soon. Eighty-two percent of sales happen after the first follow-up!

7. **Trying to Be Cute and Funny:** Use direct response (not "Madison Avenue") advertising.

8. **BAD Copy:** The right words rule!

9. **Too Much Reliance on One Media:** Diversify! Multiple legs on table!

What drives you?

Knowing the right answer to this question can make you more money, faster and easier than you think! Here are the six main needs that "drive" all of us. The need for:

1. Variety

2. Stability

3. Love/Connection

4. Significance

5. Growth

6. Contribution

Discover the true secrets behind your most powerful motivations in life... And then look for all the ways you can fill your life with as many of these things as possible.

❧❧

Your Hour of Profit Power!

The best thing you can do to
dramatically increase your sales
and profits is to spend at least
ONE SOLID HOUR each day —
first thing in the morning — where
you think about nothing except
all the various ways you can sell
more stuff to your marketplace.

Prosperity consciousness and "new age thinking" sounds great — but most new age thinkers I know are always broke!

Why is this?

Happiness lies in the relentless pursuit of profits!

- ✓ The thrill is in the hunt, not the catch!

- ✓ Keep searching for newer and better ways to make more money!

- ✓ Turn all of your money-getting activities into a game that you play — for the sake of playing!

- ✓ Making money really is the greatest game on earth!

Street-smart business rule:
**Take good care of the people
who are taking good care of you!**

Surround yourself with the best
people you can find. <u>Then
don't</u> <u>run</u> <u>them</u> <u>off</u>!

The best employee is often a
combination of several of them.

ou can't teach people how to be wise. This is something that <u>must</u> <u>be</u> <u>earned</u> over a period of time.

- Facing all the problems — moving forward year after year — in spite of all the obstacles.

- Living through some terribly painful times.

- Discovering what you *hate* and *don't want*. (Much more important than what you do want.)

- Not giving up when any other sane and rational person would.

Manipulation can be a damn good thing.

The <u>best</u> things in my life started out being nothing more than delusions... I thank God for all the people who have lied to me about how simple and easy it would be to get rich, become a master copywriter, write books, have a happy marriage, and all the other things I have paid such a huge price for. Had I known how difficult these things were to achieve, I would have never started!

The _more_ money a customer spends — the _less_ problems they cause you.

There are exceptions to this, but they are few and far between. The BIGGEST pain in the ass customers are almost _always_ the ones who spend the least amount of money.

Not making enough money?

★ Your sales and profits are <u>not</u> high enough?

★ IT'S YOUR OWN FAULT!

★ The day you accept full responsibility for <u>all</u> the money you do or don't make is also the day you can begin to turn <u>everything</u> around.

◆ ◆ ◆

"Consumption expands with usage."

— Dan Kennedy

I used to worry that I was trying to sell too much stuff to my customers. Now I only worry that I'm not selling them enough stuff!

◆ ◆ ◆

❖ ❖ ❖

Dependable monthly income sets you free!

Especially if you don't have to do much (or even anything!) to keep it coming in!

Strive to create as <u>many</u> of these types of opportunities as possible!

❖ ❖ ❖

Massive action solves ALL personal financial problems!

- Turn up the volume!

- Start moving in 40 directions at once!

- Find the things that produce the biggest results and then repeat them in the biggest way you can!

"The closer you get to
the ultimate goal,
the less exciting it is."

— *Neil Young*

WAY
257

ne of the reasons two-step marketing works so well is it lets you "test" to see how motivated the other person is.

The <u>bigger</u> the action is you are making them take — the <u>more</u> motivated they are. (This is also the main reason that the people who spend the <u>most</u> money with you will <u>always</u> cause you the fewest problems.)

If someone you want to sell to is <u>not</u> motivated, they'll either back out of the deal or they'll make you pay later.

Even the world's greatest hypnotist (Milton Ericson) knew that you could never hypnotize somebody *unless a part of them wanted to change.* In other words, Milton knew that you can't make someone do what they don't want to do. He used all kinds of subtle hypnotic induction techniques to get past some of the thin layers of resistance, but if the layer was too thick nobody could penetrate it. (To test his theory, he once put his sister in a very deep state of hypnosis and then asked her to take her clothes off. Even though she was in a very deep trance and in the most highly suggestive state of mind possible, she immediately refused and quickly came out of hypnosis!)

Robert J. Ringer's 3 simple moneymaking rules:

1. If you want more, make yourself worth more.

2. Concentrate on quality and service <u>first</u>, and profit will automatically follow.

3. Always give people more than you expect to get in return.

   ❖ Out of these 3, I believe #1 is more important than the other 2 combined!

   ❖ The more you do to make yourself worth more (even if it is only hype and bullshit — such as writing a bunch of books!), the more money you <u>will</u> automatically make.

———∞———

Unreasonable people rule the world!

All great entrepreneurs are a bit unreasonable!

———∞———

❧

**Great entrepreneurs love change.
We embrace it! We need it.
We crave it. The rest of the world
is our <u>exact</u> opposite in this regard.**

❧

What something costs is not the issue. The only thing that matters is the profit you make.

Many times you must spend more money to make more money.

It takes more money, not less, to do the things that are necessary to completely separate yourself from all of your competitors and shock all of your best prospects and customers.

A fatal sin we all commit (even those of us who know better) is to hold back when we should be giving and doing more.

Spending more money to convert sales does not have to be risky. You can test small — and let the numbers prove that this is the better move that "will" make you more money. Only then will you commit to spending the BIG BUCKS. However, even then, you can closely monitor each campaign and STOP spending all this extra money whenever you see your profits declining.

**"There are only two things
that will make you money
in any business: marketing and
innovation. Everything else is
a business expense."**

— Management Guru, Peter Drucker

This quote should be on every business
owner's desk — on their bathroom mirror and
hanging from their rear view mirror while they
drive. Let's all beat it into our heads! Then make
sure we spend the maximum amount of time,
work, and money in both of these areas today!

WAY
263

To some degree, it's all a
numbers game. Be very
persistent and don't give up!

Remember the old sales adage,
**"Some will, some won't.
So what? Who's next?"**

Timid salespeople
raise skinny kids.

Being a lifelong entrepreneur takes a great deal of courage...

Anyone can do it on the short-term. Anyone can handle it when it's all so fresh, new, and super exciting! Or when everything is smooth sailing and things are all coming together. But to do it year in and year out — through all the peaks and valleys — with all the difficulties and challenges we face each year... that takes courage. To keep doing it <u>after</u> the thrill is gone — when it becomes "work" — when it all stops being fun — when you have to suffer and work through the hard times — when your heart gets broken because things did not turn out the way you wanted or when everything seems to be going downhill — when you think you can't take it anymore and want to quit... but keep moving forward anyway, all that takes tremendous courage. Can you relate to what I'm saying? If not, you haven't been in the game long enough or you are not demanding more from yourself and pushing it hard enough. If you can relate — all I can say is *"Keep fighting the good fight! Never surrender!"*

How to double your sales in one year:

Harry Cunningham, the man who was responsible for starting K-Mart and making it the <u>biggest</u> discount retailer in the country (before Wal-Mart took away that title!) got his start by taking over a failing store in Grosse Pointe, Michigan. He came up with this brilliantly simple plan. He asked sales clerks to note any customer requests on blue index cards. By carrying what they asked for, he doubled the store's sales in one year!

It sounds so damn simple, doesn't it? Just find out what people really want — and then give them <u>more</u> of it in a better way than everyone else is giving it to them! What could be more simple? And yet, I'll bet you'll <u>never</u> learn this in Harvard Business School.

In a perfect word, if it were possible to *really* give your customers the <u>biggest</u> thing they wanted the very most — what would it be?

Who is coming the <u>closest</u> to giving them these things right now? How can you use the best ideas from these people?

The answers to these questions will come slowly. You *must* live with these questions for a while. Keep asking them... and writing down the responses. Your answers will get better

**Victor Hugo (the great French
revolutionist) once said,
*"Those who live are
those who fight!"***

❦

He's right! The day you stop fighting
is the day you begin to die.
This is true for your life and for
the life of your business.

If you don't know it can't be done, you can do it.

An educated person will stay up all night and worry about things that most of us never even think about. We are too damn busy doing the deal to worry about anything.

Should you write naked?

I once heard a respected marketer say that he only writes copy when the moon is full. He claimed this gave him the power he needed to put the right words on paper. At first I thought he was joking. When I realized he wasn't I said out loud, "That's the stupidest thing I have ever heard!" Now I'm not so sure... You see, writing is a <u>deeply personal activity</u> and there is no one way to do it. The real secret is to experiment with many different things, find out what works best for you, and then do them on a regular basis.

Most ads and sales letters are boring as hell!

They deliver zero "sales performance." They are painful to read... there's no excitement factor... zero enthusiasm... and nothing that compels the prospect to go through the <u>time</u> and <u>trouble</u> to read it.

The **why** to do something always
comes before the **how** to do it!
This is the secret behind all great achievers.

Great achievers set the goal —
and then figure it out as they go along.
You can't let a little thing like not knowing how
you're going to do something stop you!

❖·❖·❖

Diversity in your
marketing leads to
stability in your business.
Hit 'em hard. Hit 'em
often. **Hit 'em many
different ways!**

❖·❖·❖

66 The writer who gets things done is the writer who shows up for work day in and day out... Regular hours and regular production are the keys to productivity. The hare may show a lot of early form, but the smart money's always on the tortoise. **99**

— Lawrence Block from the book,
"Telling Lies For Fun And Profit"

<u>Never</u> <u>Fear</u> <u>Objections</u>.

Don't hide! Be upfront about
the skepticism you know they
feel... Bring up the biggest
objections yourself. Then overcome
them one by one. You'll win their
trust and respect — and
you'll get their money.

*The best prospects have major
objections that must be faced
head-on and not skated around.*

THE SECRET OF SELF-PROMOTION:

YOU ARE WHO YOU SAY YOU ARE!

Niche Marketing:

Spending <u>more</u> money
to reach fewer people.
Fewer people that are highly
qualified and more likely to buy.

The path of least resistance leads to a life of mediocrity. But, when given two choices — people will always take that path. They'll always take the easiest way... It's human nature.

Test small, *but aggressively.*

You can lose money
on 9 out of 10 tests and
<u>still</u> make millions by
rolling out the 1 winner!

◈ ◈ ◈

You'll never find your greatest winners without aggressive testing.

Every new customer
is an investment
toward future profits!

Nothing great was never accomplished by business owners whose goal was "slow controlled growth."

We have the power to influence the people we sell to!

Our success is not dependent on the market we serve — nearly as much as it is in our ability to know how to continually give this market what they want.

Get the word 'problem' out of your vocabulary...

There's no such thing as problems — *there are only opportunities and challenges!*

The pain of discipline
hurts <u>less</u> than
the pain of regret.

Make your high
price seem cheap —
by comparing it
against something
much more expensive!

Forbes Ley says that the
#1 reason people buy almost
anything and everything
is because somehow they
believe it will help them feel
better about themselves.

——— $ $ $ ———

Relationship Marketing:

Win their hearts — then win their pocketbooks!

——— $ $ $ ———

Motivation is an internal thing. <u>Nobody can give it to you</u>.

You must keep looking for reasons to win!

"Man inhabits a
world of delusion."

— *Edward De Ropp*

People buy cures — not prevention.

They'll spend their life-savings on a wild cure, but little or nothing on prevention.

The wise marketer sees the connections between many different things.

Test everything!

Sometimes it takes a lot of wrong answers to get to the right ones.

Isn't it stupid to spend your valuable time doing the things that others can do <u>faster</u> — <u>easier</u> — and <u>better</u> than you?

People who are great
at making excuses —
are often lousy
at making money.

<u>Game Theory for Marketers</u>:

"Game Theory" is the latest buzz of
the academic community. Highly
educated people have made quite a study
of this new area. The concept is simple:
"Put yourself into a position that you
<u>don't</u> want to be in and then rescue
yourself!" In the process of doing this,
you discover <u>many</u> interesting things.
When I first read about this I said to
myself, "This is what all great
entrepreneurs have been doing since the
beginning of time!" *It's true!* We
constantly force ourselves to tap into
parts of ourselves that we don't normally
reach by constantly biting off way more
than we can chew! We back ourselves
into corners and then <u>fight</u> <u>our</u> <u>way</u> <u>out</u>!

✡✡✡✡✡✡✡✡✡

One ounce of cure will **always** outsell 1,000 pounds of prevention!

✡✡✡✡✡✡✡✡✡

If you don't take large risks,
you'll <u>never</u> make great gains.

Of course, there are plenty
of ways you can test small — *but
VERY AGGRESSIVELY!*

◆ <u>STOP</u> LOWERING ◆ YOUR PRICES!

Low prices are reserved for people who <u>cannot</u> market themselves effectively. If you're competing on price, you haven't established enough value in the minds of your prospective customers. It's up to you to prove — without a doubt — that the best prospective buyers in your market should be giving more of their money to you. Marketing is all about differentiation, but it's up to you to create those perceptions of difference in the minds of the people you most want on your customer list.

<u>Business</u> <u>is</u> <u>work</u>!

"Any commander's greatest fear is the
fear of failure. It preys on you.
You have to keep your focus. You have
to consider all the things that could go
wrong, but then you have to quickly
banish them from your mind.
If you think about them too long, you
can't go forward — you're paralyzed."

*— Robert Prince, Assault Commander
of WWII's Most Dramatic Mission*

    This quote jumped out to me because this
is the same exact principle that those of us in
business deal with every day. The risks in
business can be very dangerous. We <u>must</u>
understand all the things that could go wrong
and develop some strong back-up plans of
attack. Everything must be thought through,
but in the end we <u>must</u> bravely move forward
and attack!

◈ ◈ ◈

People <u>re-buy</u> the most by selling them the same way you sold them before.

◈ ◈ ◈

Spend <u>more</u> money to attract the <u>smaller</u> group of *the prime prospects* you most want as long-term customers.

Are all highly-successful entrepreneurs a little crazy?

Maybe, but one thing is for certain:
almost all of them tend to be very creative.
The symptoms of creativity are also
directly related to insanity!

Check it out for yourself:

CREATIVITY	MADNESS
High energy	Mania, insomnia
Heightened senses	Mood disorder
Eccentricity	Erratic behavior
Emotional expressiveness	Emotional volatility
Spontaneity	Impulsiveness
Risk taking	Recklessness
Single-mindedness	Obsessiveness
Unusual perceptions	Distortions of reality
Visions	Hallucinations
Big ideas	Grandiosity
Fluency of ideas	Flight of ideas
High standards	Perfectionism
Feelings of giftedness	Narcissism

The more you think about this,
you'll realize that all great entrepreneurs
definitely have all of the symptoms on the
left-hand side of this chart!

When you find your successful formula — <u>don't</u> <u>change</u> <u>it</u>!

...At least until the numbers start going downhill.

Until then, keep finding as many ways as you can to continue making as much money as possible with the same formula that has worked so well for you.

The role of the "visionary" in <u>every progressive company</u> is to believe it BIGGER and see it SIMPLER than ever before!

A direct mail secret.

Direct mail will bring you significantly better customers than <u>any</u> <u>other</u> <u>media</u>. This is especially true when compared to mediums such as the Internet. With direct mail you get what you pay for. Sure, it's expensive, but the end result is the fact that you end up with customers who end up being worth a whole lot more money.

Isn't this what it's all about?

If copy is king —
then readability is the queen!

If you <u>can't</u> get them to read it — nobody will buy. You <u>must</u> do everything possible to BREAK UP YOUR WRITING.

A. It must be perceived as easy to read. No BIG BLOCKS or pages of tiny fonts.

B. It must be <u>jagged</u> and <u>never smooth</u>.

C. Each page of your sales letter must somehow "look and feel" different from the preceding page.

D. You <u>must</u> do anything and everything to make it look inviting and interesting.

Involvement is the key... You must do as many things as possible to get and then keep them involved. The deeper they go — the more power you will have to convince them to give you their money.

If your customers want to buy rocks... <u>then start digging!</u>

Most marketers are trying too hard to sell people the things that <u>they</u> want to sell... **instead of just selling what their market wants to buy.**

Seasoned marketers are the <u>most</u> guilty of this. They believe their marketing skills are powerful enough to sell anything to anyone!

❦

"Certainty is hugely seductive."

— Anthony Starr

One thing people really want is certainty in an uncertain world. They want to be near someone who they feel has <u>all</u> <u>the</u> <u>answers</u>... Someone who has it all figured out and will now take care of them.

SPEED

Being *faster* is <u>more</u> <u>important</u>
than being perfect!

A half-baked idea well executed
is much better than that
"perfect" idea that is <u>always</u>
just around the corner!

Why work when you're already worth $100 million dollars?

"You have got to be, wild guess, worth somewhere north of 100 million dollars. Why are you still touring? You don't have to do this," Scott Pelley remarked in a *60 Minutes* interview with Bruce Springsteen (originally aired October 7, 2007).

"What else would I do? You got any clues?" Springsteen asks. "Got any suggestions? I mean, am I going to garden? Why would you stop. I mean, you play the music and, you know, grown men cry. And women dance. That's why you do it."

<u>The bottom line</u>: You gotta do what makes you feel most alive or most fulfilled... and then find a way to get paid a lot of money for doing it!

Do the things that scare you and you will have the power!

Once you go through the terror a bunch of times, you are not nearly as afraid!

In fact, many times your fear turns into excitement!

You simply re-direct your fearful energy and use it for all kinds of good things.

And there is no greater feeling than the one you get when you MASTER YOUR BIGGEST FEARS!

Keep hunting for your next big idea. **You never know when or where you'll find it.**

⌘

Viagra was a heart medication — still in its testing phase — when some researcher took note of a <u>very interesting side effect</u>!

>⟶⊙⟵<

A **secret** from one of the wealthiest men in history:

"There is no secret about success. Success simply calls for hard work, devotion to your business at all times, day and night."

— *Henry Clay Frick*

WAY
313

Most of the ads and sales letters being created and used are worthless!

They are too neat and clean. • They're too homogenized. • They lack any real personality. • They are created to not offend people, but end up not making any effect. • They are professional and polished — but also phony and easily ignored. • The bottom line: There is no "sales" in the sales material! • You must strive to create the exact opposite of all this worthless crap!

Your sales material must be:

Real! • Raw! • Filled with personality! • Only aimed at the exact person you are trying to reach. • Somewhat controversial. • Dramatic! • BOLD and daring! • Exciting! • Totally different! • Fun and/or interesting. • Perhaps even a bit wild and crazy or outrageous!

Your job is to completely and totally separate yourself and your company from all of the other companies in your market. **Don't hold back!** <u>STOP</u> worrying about offending people and <u>START</u> thinking about attracting the largest number of the exact types of people you want to do business with for the longest period of time. **Nothing else matters.**

ॐ ॐ ॐ

Be thankful for <u>all</u> of your burdens.

"If it were not for the things that go wrong in your work, for the difficult people you have to deal with, for the burden of the decisions you have to make, and for the responsibility you carry, a lesser person could do your job at about half of what you make."

— Nido R. Quebein
From his powerful book,
How to Get Anything You Want!

❖◇❖◇❖◇❖◇❖◇❖◇❖◇

"Warfare constantly requires adaptation and innovation."

— Richard Danzig,
Secretary to the Navy

He's right, but this is also true of business warfare!

Declare war on your competitors!

❖◇❖◇❖◇❖◇❖◇❖◇❖◇

Why most of your
competitors
are <u>EASY</u> to beat:

Most small business people are not focused on the few projects that can make them the most money. <u>They have no real game plan</u>. Some of the most ambitious ones are very busy — <u>but are not focused</u>. Because of this, they are easy to beat! All you have to do is stay focused on the small number of projects that have the ability to make you the largest amount of money in the fastest time! *Remember, it's more important to do the right things than to do things right.*

WAY
NUMBER
317

The 3 "F's" of selling
to their emotions.
Know your prospects' BIGGEST...

☞Fears,

☞Frustrations,

and

☞Failures!

Let that question burn into your brain. Spend
some time thinking about it very carefully.
Then start building your sales message around
these key areas. Don't pussyfoot around these
areas. Clearly bring all of them up and show
and tell your prospective buyers how you will
solve each one of these things for them.

NEVER abdicate your marketing.

Your marketing
(all the <u>specific</u> things you do to attract and retain customers and do the maximum amount of repeat business with them for the <u>largest</u> profit) is much too important to turn over to someone else.

There are so many consultants and freelancers who want you to "let them do it all for you." *Don't do it!*

⍥GOYA!⍥

Action generates inspiration!
The way to get more great ideas is
move! You gotta get off your ass
every day and start working on the
projects that stand the greatest
chance of making you the
LARGEST amount of money.

*It seems simple and it is simple.
Yet, how many people do
this religiously?*

What is your #1 competitive advantage?

You <u>must</u> be able to answer this question in the clearest way... *and it has to be a great answer!*

Aristotle Onassis said, "The secret to business isto know something that none of your competitors know."

Bill Glazer's...
Info-Marketing Formula:

1. Quality product.

2. Quality lead.

3. Marketing funnel (sequential follow-up mailings).

4. Risk reversal.

5. Continuity income.

6. What's next?

This simple six-step formula can make you massive sums of money!
It's a proven millionaire-maker!

*T*he <u>best</u> marketing ideas
from one industry
are easily *transferable*
to your market.

Stay open! <u>Think</u>! *Be creative!* The more
you do to expand your awareness of the fact
that ideas are transferable — the better. You
will be able to find all the ways you can add
and combine the <u>best</u> ideas that other markets
are using.

Most of your competitors are LOCKED into
their own little world. **They're about as
creative as a head of cabbage!** This makes it
easy for you to step in, do something BOLD and
new, and dominate your market!

ഃഗ

Change is the only thing that is permanent.

ഃഗ

One good golf shot wipes out a hundred bad ones!

Keep playing for that one good shot.

Why prospects <u>DON'T</u> buy right away:

1. Not enough pain with their current situation.

2. They don't perceive they have a need.

3. They can't distinguish that you're any better.

4. They don't trust you, your company, or your offer.

5. They don't trust themselves or think it will work for them.

6. You did not follow-up enough or put enough pressure on them.

Notice how "not having the money" is not on the list?

Thinking your entire marketing plan out from every angle — on paper — is a form of action.

Your best ideas will come to you while you are in the process of figuring everything out on paper. Setting your financial goals, working out projections, thinking through all of the potential challenges, and developing specific strategies to overcome the challenges.

<u>Does all this sound like work</u>? It's not. It's a game! The more you play the game — the more power you'll have!

> ## When people pay —
> ## they pay attention!
>
> *Eric J. Bechtold*

A good direct mail
package is not afraid
of the word NO!

Do you own a business or the
worst job in in the world?
Take this test to find out!

�(«») ◲ ◲

Can the business
survive and even thrive
without you?

◲ ◲ ◲

It is to the degree that you can
honestly say "YES!" to this question
that will determine whether
you in fact own a business or
just a highly paid job.

Great premiums *drive* the sale!

Make your bonuses so attractive and sound so valuable that people are willing to buy your product or service just to get the bonuses.

·· ♔ ··

The power of ROI!

It doesn't matter how much
something costs. The only thing
you should care about is
how much <u>money</u> it <u>makes</u> <u>you</u>.

Stop looking for an easier and softer way.

Remember, all progress comes from discontent, not complacency. *Stay hungry* and <u>always</u> <u>let</u> <u>your</u> <u>reach</u> <u>exceed</u> <u>your</u> <u>grasp</u>!

$$$

Start charging more money for your stuff!

Someone has to be the highest price competitor... it might as well be you!

Charging more money lets you deliver higher quality products and services that attract the very best prospects in your market.

$$$

❧Learn by doing.☙

You can't let a simple thing like the fact that you've <u>never</u> done something or don't know how to do it stop you from doing it.

The fact that entrepreneurs are willing to boldly step out and face the unknown — and figure it all out as they go — is the one thing that separates them from everyone else.

❧

Any **fool** can create and sell **products,** but it takes a true genius to create an ever-growing base of loyal fanatics who re-buy an increasing amount of products and services on a *frequent* basis.

ONE WAY is
the <u>wrong way</u>.

More choices and options is the
<u>right</u> way. Variety is power!
Flexibility is strength.

$ $ $ $ $

The more HONEST and OPEN you are with your customers, the more <u>BONDED</u> they will be to you and the more they'll buy!

People are sick and tired of all the
phony-sounding B.S. out there.
THEY DON'T TRUST ANYONE ANYMORE.
They are looking for something "<u>REAL</u>"
and want to have a relationship with you.
The more you do to tell them your carefully
crafted "personal and private" details,
the more money you'll make.

Try this and prove it to yourself!

$ $ $ $ $

**❝The Rambo types
are the first to go.❞**

*Commanding Officer
of SEALS Training at the
Naval Special Warfare Center*

The secret to survival in war or business is to be flexible and adaptable. There is no one way. You must have opposing skills and qualities that let you bend <u>without</u> breaking... You need qualities that let you take some of the most brutal beatings without smashing into a thousand pieces.

❦❧❦❧

Success is a moving target.

You have to keep chasing it!

❧❦❧❦

What are your **top 3 competitive advantages** and how can you exploit them in a bigger and better way?

Ask yourself this question, often.

Stop worrying about the cost of your leads!

I used to hang around with a group of marketers who sat around and bragged about the "low cost of leads." Each guy in the group would try to show off and give a lower number than the next guy.

BUT I <u>NEVER</u> PARTICIPATED IN THOSE CONVERSATIONS.

Why? Because the cost of the lead is no big deal! The only thing that matters is how much money you make! Sometimes your best bet is to spend more money on a lead than any of your other competitors are willing to spend. After all, the profitable conversion of the leads you generate is definitely <u>the</u> <u>most</u> <u>important</u> <u>thing</u>.

The lonely crowd.

People are "starving" for a little genuine and sincere recognition. Feed it to them and you'll get super rich!

Want proof from 2 people who knew?

"The two things people want
more than sex or money
are praise and recognition."

— *Mary Kay Ash*

"My life changed forever the
day I realized that a man
would die for a blue ribbon."

— *Napoleon Bonaparte*

Without duty... life is soft and boneless.

"I slept and dreamt that life was joy. I awoke and saw that life was duty. I acted and beheld that duty was joy."

— *Rabindranath Tagore*

Strive to be <u>more</u> "human" in all of your communications.

✓ Be real!

✓ Be raw!

✓ Be imperfect!

Let them feel what you feel and see the REAL person behind the words they are reading.

Use the carrot and the stick to get them to buy from you!

Let the twin forces of <u>positive</u> and <u>negative</u> go to work for you.

Remember, people are more likely to act to avoid pain than to move towards pleasure. So give them something to move towards, but also to move away from. *Make them feel <u>both</u> good about buying and bad about not buying.*

Surround yourself with the best and brightest your money will buy!

▦ ▦ ▦

When you hire people who are smarter than you are, you prove that you are smarter than they are!

▦ ▦ ▦

The smartest and most capable people are always working for someone else. *They might as well be working for you!*

WAY
NUMBER
347

What is the #1 financial
goal for your business
__RIGHT__ __NOW__?

You __must__ have a clear target!
A goal that excites you and causes
you to stretch and reach for more!

You <u>can't</u> kill an
elephant with a BB gun!

— *Bill Glazer*

People are trying to get HUGE
results with a small amount
of effort and expense.

YOU <u>CAN'T</u> DO IT!

So much of the slick, polished, and "professional looking" sales material is also <u>the first to hit the trash can</u>!

The marketplace is cluttered with all of this homogenized sales material. In an attempt to make it "perfect" it also comes off as being mass-produced and phony! *There is no edge to it... No personality... Nothing to suggest that a real, living, breathing person actually created it.*

★ ★ ★ ★ ★

Rock star or brain surgeon?

Your time is the most precious commodity you have. *So why would you want to sell it for any amount of money?* <u>Don't</u> <u>do</u> <u>this</u>! Find as many ways as you can to make money that have little or even nothing to do with the amount of time you put into it.

★ ★ ★

All <u>great entrepreneurs</u> are non-conformists because conformity leads to conventional results.

Conformists are people who follow the follower. Entrepreneurs are rule breakers who pave their own path.

❖ ❖ ❖

Make yourself and/or
your company so *unique*
that you completely
<u>separate</u> yourself from all
of your competitors.

Get the prospects
to seek you out!

❖ ❖ ❖

What are the BRUTAL
realities of your market
<u>that</u> <u>you</u> <u>have</u> <u>not</u>
been facing up to?

*And <u>what</u> are you going
to do about it?*

WAY
NUMBER
354

The scam of "Lifetime Customer Value:"

Many marketing professionals want you to focus on your "Lifetime Customer Value" so you <u>won't</u> think about the terrible response rates you're getting from the promotions they are putting together for you or helping you with.

It's nice to focus on big-picture concepts such as lifetime value of your customers. But too much focus on this principle will definitely lead to bankruptcy!

You #1 goal should always be getting the largest and fastest return on every dollar you spend on marketing. Once you do that — you can think of bigger picture issues.

Price resistance usually only lives in the business owner's mind.

The biggest obstacle to raising price is in the business owner's mind.

Become a ◆◆◆◆◆ marketing pitbull!

Most marketers give up on their prospective buyers way too soon. Don't do this! Be more relentless in all of your marketing efforts. Go after them in the most aggressive way — <u>and</u> <u>stay</u> <u>after</u> <u>them</u>.

◆◆◆   ◆◆◆   ◆◆◆

The ABC's of Wealth:

I started my first business in December of 1985 and called it, "ABC's Carpet and Upholstery Cleaning." I chose this name for two reasons: #1 — I wanted to be first in the phone book (a stupid idea that many other dummies believe will bring them business). #2 — I was reading a success book at the time that told me about the ABC's of success.

Those ABC's of success went like this: All you need to make all of your dreams come true is the right Attitude, a strong and unshakable Belief, and a firm Commitment. The book told me that if I had all 3 of these things I could never fail! So, because I wanted to motivate myself in the most passionate way, I made this my company name and told everyone about the ABC's of success. I was like a newborn Christian who is out to save the world!

Years later I stopped believing in the ABC's formula. I thought it was way too simplistic. I laughed at myself for ever accepting such a stupid idea. I learned a million things about business and marketing, made a lot of money, and felt sorry for all of those poor "self-help addicts" who put all their hope in such silly mantras. I felt proud and superior.

But now, more than 20 years later, I have come full circle. I see that the true secret to getting and staying rich (and not losing your soul in the process) is finding the right combination of specific business building knowledge, skills, and even things as simple and brilliant as this ABC formula!

Don't be too cheap when it comes to buying customers.

✓ Every customer <u>must</u> <u>be</u> <u>bought</u>... but most marketers are trying to do this as cheaply as possible.

✓ New customer acquisition is an investment towards future profits. This is one area of your marketing where you really need to be consistently BOLD!

✓ All of your profits come from doing more business with your current customers, but new customers are still the life-blood of your business! <u>You must build the most aggressive marketing system possible</u> — that can consitantly bring you the largest number of new customers. Do all this right and you will have a powerful marketing advantage over your competitors.

✓ So what is an aggressive new customer acquisition program? Simple. Often it means losing some money on the initial sale. This scares most people and can be very risky, but it can also produce great rewards!

Having thousands of powerful direct mail sales letters (and the follow-up sales material that goes out after you generate the leads) is like having a GIANT ARMY of the very best salespeople who <u>never complain</u>... <u>always deliver</u> their best performance... and <u>never ask for a raise</u>!

❧Screw fear!☙

Fear is the enemy of all success. It can have some positive benefits (fear of bankruptcy or prison!), but most of the time all it does is hold people back and stop them from getting the best of everything that could and should be theirs.

" I'm grateful to audiences for watching me and for enjoying what I do — but I'm not one of those who believe that a successful entertainer is made by the public, as is so often said. You become successful, the way I see it, only if you're good enough to deliver what the public enjoys. If you're not, you won't have any audience; so the performer really has more to do with his success than the public does. **"**

Johnny Carson from a December 1967
Playboy Magazine Interview

This is one of the most powerful marketing concepts you will ever learn and master. The things that people want and need are usually the opposite of each other. So it's up to us marketers to create offers that contain the appearance of giving them what they really want, while also containing the things we know they need the most.

To the average prospect — there is nothing more worthless than a sales pitch. *Most people will go out of their way to avoid a salesman who is trying to sell them something.*

To the average prospect — salespeople are a dime a dozen. They are worthless.

Because of this, the last thing you should ever want is to be perceived as a salesperson.

What people do want and place great value on are celebrities and experts who command confidence. Once you create that position in their minds, you will have the attractor factor that draws them to you.

Develop educated-based
marketing messages
and strive to be known
as a trusted adviser.

❊ ❊ ❊

Everyone wants to do
business with an expert.
Re-invent yourself to be
seen as the foremost expert
in your area and they'll stand
in line with money in hand.

PAIN is part of the process.

Embrace it...

Deal with it...

Even learn to enjoy it!

Feed the positive dog!

So what in the world does this have to do with marketing and business? Simply this: Jon Gordon tells the metaphoric story of the seeker who journeys to the mountain to see the wise man about a major problem that is bothering him greatly. He tells the guru that he feels that inside of him are two dogs: one is loving, gentle, easily excitable, totally loyal, and friendly in every way and the other one is always fearful, can be greedy, angry, lazy, and very vicious whenever he feels threatened. He tells the wise man that his entire life has been a constant struggle between these two dogs that he genuinely feels live inside of him — and he is going crazy!

The wise man listens carefully, then pauses for a long time. (Wise men do this, you know! Even if it's all for the show!) Then the wise man simply says, "Feed the positive dog!"

This is a cool metaphor! Great visual, terrific meaning, and — as you know — business forces us to deal with so many of the situations in life that most people either consciously or unconsciously try to avoid. There are many problems and challenges that we must get through and solve. It can be very difficult and it totally stretches us — sometimes beyond the breaking point. You discover over a period of time that you must be like a fine-tuned machine in order to deal with all of the B.S. that comes at you. If not — you will burn out fast and be totally worthless and ineffective.

Wisdom from the founder
of *Modern Advertising*:

"Ask a person to take a chance on you, and you have a fight. Offer to take a chance on him, and the way is easy.

I have always taken chances on the other fellow. I have analyzed my proposition until I made sure that he had the best end of the bargain. Then I had something that people could not well neglect.

I have been robbed plenty, but the robbery cost me ten times less than trying to enforce any safe proposition."

— Claude Hopkins
(On why giving away free samples
and taking other actions to invest in
the prospect first, before you ask
for their money is so important.)

Good judgment comes from experience — and experience comes from bad judgment.

Make more mistakes... faster... and learn from them.

The REAL breakfast of champions is not Wheaties cereal...

It's getting up early every morning while
the rest of the world is still asleep
and putting in 3 or 4 hours of the most
intense and focused work!

Why don't more people do this?

<u>Simply this</u>: It's too painful!
And yet, when you eat a little bit of this pain
on a daily basis, you grow very strong!

What you sell must appear to be very hard to get — but super easy to buy!

The more you can do to create the illusion that what you have to offer would be extremely difficult for them to get without you, your company, and/or whatever you offer — the better.

Build your case! Prove to them that what you have is extremely difficult and very hard or even impossible to get on their own. Apply the pressure... Make them see and feel it! Then and only then should you make it very easy for them to buy.

The power of good management:

I was talking with my general manager about a new promotion we just started. The initial response to our lead generation was exciting! With only a minimum push we had 248 fresh leads! And because I forced them to listen to a 21-minute message that pre-sold them on our offer, I was certain they were well qualified. And yet, when I asked her about the initial sales conversion, she told me that the sales reps were not very excited. Then she said one of the smartest things I have heard in a while: "Sometimes if the sales reps get 3 or 4 bad calls in a row, they think the whole list sucks!" I about drove my car off the road! You see, in all my years, I have <u>never</u> heard the problem stated so clearly. And this also points to the golden solution: That it is up to management to work with the sales force and show them that their emotions often lie. They may give up on a prospect list way too soon. Or, the fact that they believe that a list of prospective buyers is no good will greatly influence their own performance.

Good management brings the power and clarity of objectivity to the table, and that makes all the difference in the world! You can only see things clearly when you have the ability to pull back. Salespeople and/or entrepreneurs who are too close to the situation will <u>never</u> be able to see the full truth.

Give away a small piece of the
LARGER THING you want
to ultimately sell to them.

∞∞∞

Give away your <u>BEST</u> <u>STUFF</u> —
then upsell the hell out of them!

You are only looking for the few who "can" and "will" — rather than the larger number who "can't" and "won't."

The power of the intangible.

★ Master salespeople <u>always</u> focus on selling the intangible aspects of our products or services. This takes a greater degree of skill — but the increase in revenue can be huge!

★ The intangible aspects of many products and services is where the real money is to be made. The dream will <u>always</u> transcend the reality. So sell the dream! The hope! The promise! Paint the picture BIG... and BRIGHT!

★ Never be afraid to over-hype your offers. Turn up the volume full blast. The minute you think you have gone too far means you probably still have a ways to go.

Why we <u>don't</u> get the sales conversions we want:

1) Prospect is not qualified enough.

   — This is the #1 problem. The rest of the items on the list are not prioritized.

2) There is not a good enough reason to cause them to buy now!

3) The back-end offer is not related closely enough to your initial sale.

4) You tried to move them too far too fast.

   — In other words, you asked new prospects and/or very skeptical customers to give you too much money, too quickly.

5) There was no "irresistible" offer.

6) You gave up on them too soon!

   — In other words, you did not do enough follow-up marketing.

7) Poor salesmanship!

   — You simply did a lousy job of selling them — and did not do enough to prove to them that what you had to offer was worth far more than the money you were asking for in exchange.

That's it!

**"When I'm one of 'them'
I have credibility."**

— *David Lupberger*

One of the
**BIGGEST
CHALLENGES**
in business today is
eliminating all of the
distractions and
interruptions that drain us
of our <u>energy</u> and keep us
from <u>focusing</u>.

WAY
NUMBER
377

The two enemies of the
entrepreneurial life:

✂ PEACE and COMFORT. ✂

Entrepreneurs thrive under pressure!
We need new challenges. New obstacles.
New problems to solve. These things
spur us into action and it is through the
actions we take that everything great is
achieved.

You must remain disturbed! Stay angry
and restless! Embrace all of the problems
— frustrations — and confusion! Let the
pain of these seemingly negative
situations drive you forward!

The thing I hate most is when somebody
tells me to "take it easy." I hate that! If
they keep doing this I will finally get in
their face and scream, "I'll take it easy
when I'm dead!"

EMOTIONAL EMPOWERMENT

The negative emotions are a vital part of our human nature. Stop suppressing them — and start re-focusing them. They contain a tremendous amount of energy — <u>if you use them correctly</u>. Like fire, they can burn down your house (with you inside) or they can keep you alive on the coldest winter day. Your choice. But when you suppress them — you lose all of the amazing energy they contain to keep you in the game.

ANGER = Determination.

GREED = Ambition.

LUST = Machismo.

FEAR = Caution and power.

ENVY = Positive revenge.

HATE = Competitive power.

FEAR (also) = Amazing bursts of energy and excitement!

WAY
NUMBER
379

Gary Halbert used to say:

"You'll always achieve more through movement than meditation."

It never ceases to amaze me at the way the ideas flow to me after I get through an extremely difficult project that caused me so much pain and confusion. Getting past that short-term nightmare is like blowing up the dam!

You must become and remain your #1 fan!

Business can be a sad and lonely trip. You must continue to believe in yourself when nobody else does. This will empower you to keep getting back up every time you get knocked down.

Take your business to the next level.

▣ How can you serve it up even <u>better</u> than everyone else?

▣ What are the BIGGEST PROBLEMS in your market that none of your competitors are solving? *How can you solve them?*

▣ Look for problems in your market. Talk with your best customers and prospects.

Pain, problems, challenges, obstacles, heartbreak, disappointment, and setbacks are good!

In fact, you must have more of them!

Adversity of all kinds contains raw emotional
power that you can use to fuel your inner fire!
The key is to remind yourself of this —
as you are in the middle of it all.
During those times, you must
SLAP YOURSELF IN THE FACE
and snap out of it!

Let them spur you on to the right actions!

❧

**Wealth-making wisdom from an
oil tycoon who knew:**

"The more wells you drill,
the greater chance you
have of finding oil."

— H.L. Hunt

Fast was never fast enough for
H.L. Hunt. "Drill, drill, drill!"
was his company's mantra.

—⁓❦⁓—

So what? Who cares?
What's in it for me?

These are three things that people are unconsciously thinking as they're reading your copy or listening to your sales pitch.

As you are editing your material, you should go over it with the same 3 questions in your head. Then cut <u>anything</u> that doesn't answer those questions in the clearest and boldest way.

—⁓❦⁓—

"Remember, we are dealing with people who are unpredictable. What they demand one year they may disdain the next."

— Emma Bailey (1962)

◈ She goes on to say, "Something which brought high prices five years ago may go begging now!"

◈ Emma wrote this in 1962, but it's <u>even more true</u> in today's crazy world of heavy competition and instant result-seeking prospects.

◈ Promotions that brought in a ton of profits last quarter may totally bomb a few short months later!

Every time you see any successful business — you know that at one time someone made a courageous decision! They took the leap of faith! *They decided to go for it, despite the obstacles and the challenges!*

Ronald Regan said that entrepreneurs are the forgotten heroes. *He was right!* **Entrepreneurs are heroes because:**

(1) We gladly accept and even look for new ventures that are filled with risk and uncertainty.

(2) We boldly move forward in spite of all the unusual questions and the threat of failure.

(3) We face a great deal of adversity that turns other men into whimpering puppies!

(4) We are excited to move in new directions without knowing what lies before us.

(5) We keep moving forward in spite of all the obstacles and challenges that would cause most people to retreat!

(6) We keep doing whatever comes next — no matter how difficult it is!

(7) When we tackle one new area, we do not sit back for long. Now we look for other new areas to attack and conquer.

Research is what you are doing when <u>you</u> <u>don't</u> <u>know</u> what you're doing!

Your level of <u>success</u>
is determined by your
ability and *capacity*
to handle large amounts
of uncertainty.

Outrageous marketing tip:

"When in doubt, make a fool of yourself. There is a microscopically thin line between being brilliantly creative and acting like the most gigantic idiot on earth. So what the hell, leap!"

— Cynthia Heimel

Cynthia is right! Most of us are way too afraid to push the envelope. We hold back. We fear going over the top — but our marketing messages are as boring as mud.

There really is a thin line between being brilliantly creative and acting like a complete idiot!

Upsell strategy: The best time to get someone to say "YES!" to you is right after they say "YES!" to you about something else!

This is the single greatest time they are the most open and receptive to doing whatever you want them to do. Their checkbook is open and they're handing you the pen!

The bottom line speaks the *loudest!*

WAY
NUMBER
392

A friendship built around the business is a hell of a lot better than a business that's built around a friendship.

(The former can work — while the latter seldom does.)

WAY
NUMBER
393

SEVEN REASONS you should hold more
seminars, workshops, bootcamps, or other
events for your customers.

1) These events keep you involved with your customers.
   You're with them face-to-face, eyeball-to-eyeball, belly-to-
   belly. This helps you stay focused on your market.

2) It lets your customers get the feeling that you are
   somewhat accessible and can be trusted. Many marketers
   hide from their customers. Not you.

3) Even your customers who will never attend one of your
   seminars or workshops will still get the feeling that you
   are the real deal and can be trusted.

4) These events are great product-development vehicles.
   One seminar that you hold one time can easily be
   packaged into a product you can sell for many years!

5) They are great revenue generators. Lots of ways to make
   instant money selling these events. As a "product" they
   have many extremely marketable advantages, such as a
   sense of urgency to respond NOW!

6) They are good for building relationships with Joint Venture
   Partners. First, the easiest Joint Venture to do is hold a
   seminar and let other marketers come and sell their stuff.
   Second, they give you the chance to spend quality time
   with your Joint Venture Partners and build your
   relationship with them.

7) Seminars and workshops have a super-high perceived
   value. Many marketers charge thousands of dollars for
   their seminars. And people can easily see that just one or
   two ideas they can get during these highly specialized and
   focused events could be the little spark that starts the
   mighty fire for them.

WAY
NUMBER
394

✿

The CREATIVE BLOWOUT!

The creative mind feeds off variety!
It can be a little crazy at times (or
all the time!), but you must have
many projects going at the same
time. Be willing to suffer through
the pain of being overwhelmed,
frustrated, and confused. *It's okay
to feel these things!* No matter how
bad it feels, <u>nobody</u> <u>ever</u> <u>died</u> <u>from</u>
<u>the</u> <u>intense</u> <u>pain</u> <u>of</u> <u>confusion</u> <u>or</u>
<u>frustration</u>!

RISK is the price <u>you</u> <u>pay</u> for *opportunity*.

⚭⚭⚭

The beauty of this is its simplicity. If the plan gets too complex something always goes wrong.

— Walter (John Goodman)
in "The Big Lebowski"

❖ ❖ ❖

It's good to be rich!

"He that is without money may as well be buried in a rice tub, with his mouth sewn shut."

— *Chinese Proverb*

Can you be any more graphic than being buried in a rice tub with your mouth sewn shut? No! And to think this was written many hundreds of years ago!

❖ ❖ ❖

CREATIVITY and BUSINESS.

- Most people would never think of business as a creative pursuit. And most businesses aren't! In fact, most businesses are as boring as mud!

- But a few visionary entrepreneurs continue to show us that it does not have to be this way. These people make business fun and exciting for all of their customers.

◇◇◇◇◇◇◇◇◇◇◇◇◇◇◇

Let the **numbers** tell you what to do.

◇◇◇◇◇◇◇◇◇◇◇◇◇◇◇

Winning isn't everything...
but losing
REALLY SUCKS!

A great Dorothea Brande quote from her 1936 book, "Wake Up and Live!":

"Usually, far from overrating our abilities, we do not understand how great they are. The reason for this under-estimation of ourselves will be considered later, but it is well to realize that few except the truly insane believe themselves suited for careers far beyond their full powers."

Do you have to be crazy to succeed in the biggest possible way? <u>Maybe</u>! So go crazy!
Set goals that are higher than anything
you can imagine. Who knows,
you might just grow into them.

Or in an outrageous attempt to achieve these goals, you could set off in a whole new direction you would have never imagined had you not decided to THINK and ACT bigger.

Wisdom from New York's BIGGEST thinker

— Donald Trump
from The Art of the Deal:

"People think I'm a gambler. I've never gambled in my life. To me, a gambler is someone who plays slot machines. I prefer to own slot machines! It's a good business being the house... If you go for a home run on every pitch, you're going to strike out a lot. I try never to leave myself too exposed, even if it means sometimes settling for a triple, a double, or even, on rare occasions, a single."

A major part of all success can simply be boiled down to the willingness to do what everyone around you is unwilling or unable to do.

If you're looking for a secret you can fit on a 3" x 5" index card —
THERE IT IS!

Most entrepreneurs don't think
BIG enough... They waste $1,000
worth of time and energy on a
$100 problem.

> *Don't do this!* Keep your eye on
> the prize! Be willing to walk
> over many $100.00 bills to get
> to the millions!

♥ ♥ ♥

What about love and money?

When I look at the times I made the most money in the shortest periods of time, it was when I was totally in love with what I was doing. This is the moneymaking power nobody talks about. **You must fall passionately in love with your business or at least the parts of it that bring you the most money. *Love is power!*** You are most alive when you're in love and — because of this — you will find a way to do amazing things that you couldn't begin to ever do without this awesome invisible power.

⁂

Most advertising <u>sucks</u>!

"The advertising business is going down the drain. It's being pulled down by the people who create it, who don't know how to sell anything, who have never sold anything in their lives... who despise selling, whose mission in life is to be clever show-offs and con clients into giving them money to display originality and genius."

— *David Ogilvy*

The experience of taking something from your head, putting it on paper, sending it out, and then bringing in millions of dollars has to be one of the greatest feelings on earth!

🌱

Talk about the power of manifestation. Wow!
This is alchemy in action!

Let this be your guiding mantra:

"Your job is to go as far as you
can see. You will then see
far enough to go further."

— *Brian Tracy*

The single greatest quality of the
entrepreneur is the courage to
dream BIG dreams and dare to move
forward — with only the haziest idea
of how it's all going to come together!

⚜

Educational marketing is the best way to deliver any sales message because:

1. It lets the best prospective buyers seek you out.

2. It empowers those buyers by making it appear as if it were <u>their</u> <u>choice</u> to come to you.

3. It lowers their sales resistance and lets them "sell themselves" on you, your company, or your products and services.

4. It makes people want to do business with you! They come to you ready, willing, and able to pay the premium prices you charge.

In short, this form of marketing makes the best prospective buyers in your market think and feel that it is <u>their</u> <u>choice</u> to do business with you. *They come to you already sold!*

Success leaves clues and when you study the lives of all super-successful people — you will discover that they never did it by themselves. **There was always a group of people behind and sometimes in front of them — every step of the way.**

It's the unique combination of the talents, skills, experience, support, and guidance of all of those people that made the biggest difference. Without these people — and everything they brought to the table — the "superstar" at the top would have never made it. *Or at least they would have never made it on such a grand scale.*

இலைஜ

Answers <u>come</u> <u>from</u> <u>action</u>!

Want more answers? *Take more action!* In fact, you must take MASSIVE ACTION! Move in a thousand directions! Test a million things as fast as you can. *Move damn it, move!*

WAY
NUMBER
412

⊡ ⊡ ⊡ ⊡ ⊡

The killer disease of the 21st Century:

"Information OVERLOAD!"

People are absolutely positively
OVERWHELMED with too much information...
and they can't take one more idea or sales
pitch! Many salespeople and marketers
confuse information with communication.
They try to tell them too much, too fast,
and it's all information that means something
to the marketer but it's <u>not</u> <u>necessarily</u>
<u>perceived</u> <u>as</u> <u>IMPORTANT</u> to the prospect.

⊡ ⊡ ⊡ ⊡ ⊡

14 QUESTIONS in every prospective
buyer's head that you must answer in the right
way or lose the sale:

1. Who are you?

2. What do you do?

3. How do you do it?

4. Why does what you do or advocate matter?

5. Why should I listen to you?

6. How are you different?

7. Why do I need you?

8. Who else have you worked with?

9. How long will it take?

10. What if I'm not happy?

11. How much will it cost?

12. How do I know I can trust you?

13. Why should I do this now?

14. What's the worst that can happen to me if I
    don't do it?

*The best prospects feel they have seen and heard it
all a thousand times before!* Find and develop unique
ways to answer all 14 of those questions... and the sale
is yours!

Start buying <u>more</u> <u>stuff</u>...
◈RIGHT NOW!◈

The more stuff you buy — the more money you can make! I'm serious. This is not a joke. If you truly want to crawl inside of the minds and hearts of your average prospective buyer — you must continue to buy the same stuff that he or she is buying! Or at least buy as many things as possible (via direct response marketing) from an ultra-competitive marketplace where each company must chase after you!

When you buy a lot of stuff from the market you sell to — or an active marketplace that you are very interested in – you re-experience the RUSH and the THRILL of buying! You begin to remember how it feels to be a rabid buyer! Or if you never have been a rabid buyer — you experience it for the first time. This is an important key to fully understanding the emotional side of the marketing process. By doing this, you begin to put yourself into the shoes of the people you sell to. Buy enough stuff and you will (hopefully) become a rabid buyer yourself! *This will make you a much better marketer!*

The best marketers are always the ones who are the most relentless in their follow-up activities. Once they attract a highly qualified prospect, they <u>don't</u> give up! They stay after them. They bug the hell out of them. **They try to do anything and everything they can to get the sale!**

<u>BOTTOM LINE</u>: Most marketers give up way too soon. And because of it, they leave a lot of money on the table that could and should be theirs.

─────❧────

A good headline will always answer the question:

"What's in it for me?"

Go back and read your headlines and body copy
with the attitude of "So what?" or "Who cares?"
Be as apathetic or skeptical as you possibly can.
Then make changes accordingly.

─────❧────

"The potential problem is always the same: Can you sell it, and at what price for how long?"

— Paul MacAvoy,
Yale Economics Professor

This quote jumped off the page because I've never heard such simple words that were more true from a college professor! I was shocked! It seems so simple, and yet all entrepreneurs suffer from the fact that we fall in love with what we are doing and are blinded by our passion. We tend to suffer from the delusion that just because we love something — then so will many other people.

<u>Mantra of the visionary leader</u>:

"If I'd asked people what they wanted, they would have asked for a better horse."

— Henry Ford

This whole idea that we must "ask the customer what they want and listen closely" is a load of crap! People buy in an emotional vacuum. The only way to know what they really want is to test a lot of different things and then watch the numbers closely. Then develop new products and services around the things they bought the most (while continuing to test and track the results).

From master marketing guru
Russ von Hoelscher:

"Whatever tugs at their <u>heart</u> also tugs at their <u>wallet</u>!"

Russ said these words to me when we were talking about the importance of coming up with a great emotional story behind every offer you make. The more <u>real</u>, <u>raw</u>, and <u>true</u> this story is — *the more money you will make!*

A good metaphor is a shortcut to instant understanding.

- Mastering the art of metaphors will help you sell more stuff to more people. This is your ultimate tool for making complicated things very simple.

- The key is to find the most powerful comparisons that your prospect can relate to.

WAY

421

The people you surround yourself with are EVERYTHING.

I hope you know this. I t's not just some sweet-sounding words. The right people can be worth a <u>HUGE</u> and <u>GROWING</u> <u>FORTUNE</u> to you!

You must find people who have these qualifications:

1. They are very smart.

2. They care deeply about themselves... their family and future... and you and your business.

3. They are stable and honest!

4. They have complementary skills and abilities.

5. They are long-term players who see the big picture.

6. They are teachable and willing to do whatever it takes.

7. And they must be likeable! Yes, you must like... and even love them! The more you care deeply about them and enjoy working with them (hopefully they feel the same way) – the more money you will both end up making!

In the end, the money is nice — and even vital to our businesses — *but surrounding yourself with the right people is priceless.*

A big fat lie that <u>you</u> have bought into.

A lot of businesspeople have bought into the idea that stress is bad or dangerous... But that is a lie! Yes, we have all been lied to and didn't even know it. Stress is a good and necessary thing. It's <u>strain</u> that kills — <u>not</u> <u>stress</u> (remember that). This is important because you must push yourself harder! The stress is a great thing! Just be sure you pull back... rest... and re-charge. Too much stress without plenty of intervals of rest leads to strain.

*So many people who believe that
"stress is bad" never push themselves
hard enough and never achieve the
success that could be theirs.*

This is brilliant!

When asked how he dealt with the 14 years of
drought in his career when nobody was calling...
and the parts he was being offered SUCKED...
John Travolta said, "I never stopped believing
in myself — no matter what other
people said about me or my future."

★ ★ ★

In fact, when I heard that John said this —
I instantly recognized it as oneof <u>the</u> <u>most</u>
<u>important</u> qualities that all of the
great entrepreneurs possess.

WAY
NUMBER
424

> "Advertising is what you do when you can't go see somebody. That's all it is."
>
> — *Fairfax Cane*

All we are doing is trying to the best of our ability to replace a live salesperson. We are using our sales materials and strategies to replace part or all of what a live salesperson does.

Albert Einstein once said, "If I can't see it —
I don't understand it."

This was brilliant!

Let this quote from Einstein be your wake up call to do
everything you can to make your best prospects see what
you want them to see!

How will you make them see it? Here are a few ideas:

1. Add more charts and examples.

2. Show before-and-after comparisons or
    problem/solution charts that perfectly illustrate the
    advantages you offer.

3. Tell more stories! Tell stories that move people
    emotionally. Stories that make it easy for them to
    say, think, or feel: "That's me!"

4. Use more metaphors and analogies that compare the
    things they know about with the main benefits and
    advantages of whatever you're selling.

5. Utilize more video! Let them click onto your
    Internet movies and watch — rather than read.

6. Offer them the chance to participate in activities that
    make them feel connected and involved.

Does all of this sound way too hard? Maybe, but
consider the end reward. Imagine how great it will feel if
you were to INSTANTLY double your sales and profits in the
next 60 days. *Wouldn't that be great?* Go ahead... Picture
yourself doing this — RIGHT NOW!

The days of trying to make
money in direct-response
marketing without using sales
professionals — to follow-up
and close sales — <u>is</u> <u>over</u>!

*It is amazing to me that we were
able to run our business without salespeople
for so many years...*

Even more amazing that others are <u>still</u>
trying to make it without salespeople who
follow up, close (with more pressure),
and build the all-important personal
relationships that make all of the
upselling and re-selling so much faster,
easier, and more profitable.

Obstacles are the things you see
when you take your eyes off
your goals.

⊙ <u>Stay</u> <u>focused</u>!

⊙ What are your primary goals
that are most important to you?
What are you doing TODAY to
achieve those goals in the
BIGGEST way?

⊙ You <u>must</u> have a clear and
compelling answer to that
question.

One of my favorite quotes came from the transcripts of a speech that Ernest Holmes gave in the early 1900s:

I used to think that other men were great — then I got off of my knees!

I read that quote — loved it — and tattooed it deep into my brain! And I realized this simple truth: it is wrong to place too much importance on anyone. See the greatness in certain qualities they have or in certain actions they take, but never think of them as great.

Do EVERYTHING you can to make sure you are a welcome guest instead of an annoying pest!

> Make it feel that <u>they</u> came to you instead of you going to them!

> People hate to be <u>sold</u> anything, but they love to <u>buy</u>!

> The key: *You must do all you can to make it feel as if it was their choice and not yours!*

✳✳✳

The secret of success can be as simple as building your entire business around the ultimate lifestyle you most want to live.

Simple... but not easy. Of course, all of the most <u>fulfilling</u> things in life and business are also the ones that tend to be the most difficult (at least part of the time).

✳✳✳

"THINKING BIG" has become a catchphrase for many entrepreneurs, but "THINKING BROAD" is something almost nobody talks about. It's just as important — if not more important.

What is thinking broadly all about?

Thinking broadly is all about trying to think things through from as many angles as possible, thinking conceptually, and looking at your business from the top down (instead of from the bottom up). You must see the "connections" that others can't see.

The key to making the largest amount of back-end profits is to OVER-DELIVER on your front-end fulfillment!

BLOW THEIR MIND! Make them say, "Holy crap! I can't believe they gave me so much stuff (or such a great deal)!" Then — when you offer them your back-end package — they'll buy like crazy!

(O)ne of the keys to becoming a great marketer is to put as much distance as you can between yourself and the day-to-day grind of your business.

- Hire the most competent people you can find to run your day-to-day operations. Treat them well (including pay) and then let them take care of this vital but boring and energy-zapping part of your business.

- Then, think of your company as if it were a product on a shelf and market it accordingly.

Confusion, frustration, pressure, and other varieties of emotional pain are a vital part of the business-building process. But, many entrepreneurs — including myself — suffer way too much from them. One of the BIGGEST REASONS is that we spend too much time trying to discover and develop the perfect solution without carefully thinking about all of the problems and challenges.

So stop suffering unnecessarily. Spend some quality time sharpening the ax <u>before</u> you chop away at the huge obstacles that are in your way:

1. Make a list of all of the problems and challenges you are faced with.

2. Ask yourself: What am I really trying to accomplish? What's most important? Our ideas will ultimately fail unless they are focused around the things that are most important.

3. Write it all down. Keep growing lists. Work closely with people you trust and respect who also understand your business and all of the problems, challenges, and opportunities.

4. Separate yourself from the process. Try to maintain some degree of objectivity. Remind yourself that <u>none</u> of the problems that are currently driving you crazy will matter in 50 — or even 5 — years!

Take your work seriously, but DON'T take yourself seriously. Make a game out of solving all of the problems that come at you. Think of all of these never-ending problems as the opposing team that you must defeat *in order to win the championship!*

WAY
435

> # Power perceived is power <u>achieved</u>!
>
> Enter the room like you own the place! Always hold your head high and confidently demand that they give you their money!

Facts can hide the truth.

And they can tell almost any story you want to tell.

WAY
NUMBER
437

Ralph Waldo Emerson said that "To be great is to be misunderstood." I have always loved this quote because I am an egomaniac! I'm sure other egomaniacs also have no problem believing in their own greatness!

But beyond all of this foolishness is a REAL REASON why great people are misunderstood: It is their level of commitment. They are so fully committed to what they are doing that other people just don't get it. In fact, other "normal" people think of super-successful people as "obsessive" or "compulsive" or "fanatical" or "unreasonable." Why? Because they are fully committed and engaged in all they are doing in an attempt to achieve their biggest goals and dreams.

Successful people are misunderstood because they throw their entire selves into everything they do. They don't know when to stop! Other people take one look at all of the things they are doing and think they are being totally unreasonable in every way! There must be something wrong with these people — because "they're totally obsessed with what they're doing and won't stop!" Or, they are "totally out of balance." But what normal people see as abnormal is bullshit! These super-successful people are simply paying the price they must pay to achieve the things that they want the most.

Persistence is the <u>one</u> <u>key</u> <u>factor</u> that separates those who consistently achieve phenomenal success from all the others.

It sounds simple, because it is! And yet, it works like magic!

Bottom line: You must be like one of those mean little bulldogs that grabs a hold of their pants and refuses to let go!

There is some REAL SCIENTIFIC PROOF that it pays to be persistent. One study discovered that after four attempts you have a 20% success ratio.

After four more attempts you have a 50% chance of achieving your outcome.

And after four more — you get a 70% chance of success!

And 3 more attempts gives you a 90% success rate!

Bottom line: Persistence is the key to winning big! And yet, most people give up way too soon. In fact, as many as 80% <u>quit</u> after their FIRST attempt!

All of the best salespeople and marketers are persistent. We don't give up! Once we are convinced that we have a really good prospective buyer, we do not let go! We stay after them! We crank up the pressure! We keep coming at them in as many different ways as we possibly can. We refuse to accept "no" for an answer!

Refusing to accept "no" for an answer SEPARATES you from everyone else. The secret is to come at the prospective buyer in as many different ways as you possibly can — but always do it from the position that you have something they really want that can make a dramatic difference in their lives. You're never trying to "get" something from them — you're always trying to give them what you <u>know</u> <u>for</u> <u>a</u> <u>fact</u> will give them something they really want.

Keep finding fresh, new, and creative ways to keep the pressure on!

Remember: 90% succeed after the 15th attempt, and yet 80%

You'll <u>never</u> do great things by focusing on your limitations.

Instead, you must channel all of your energy into the possibilities.

❧❦❧

"Everything you want is on the other side of your comfort zone."

— Ted Ciuba

WAY
441

You can't cost-cut your way to prosperity.

Many business owners spend way too much time focusing on cutting expenses. The problem: Whatever you focus on expands! The more expenses they cut — the more they want to cut. Then they keep cutting back <u>until</u> <u>they</u> <u>don't</u> <u>have</u> <u>a</u> <u>business</u> <u>anymore</u>!

Your main focus must ALWAYS be on increasing your sales and profits. Think offensively 70% of the time and defensively the other 30%. This will keep your focus where it must be to build your business and keep it super profitable.

"Can money make you happy?"

—∽∽—

This is an age-old question and my answer is: **"It can!"**

Here's how: The Nobel Prize winner Bertrand Russell once said: "Anything you're good at contributes to your happiness." And all of the greatest entrepreneurs I know of are really good at making money! They love the game of making money! It's the hunt... The thrill of the chase... These people are at their best when they are chasing an exciting dream or idea or vision. They love the challenge of trying to figure everything out and plowing through the obstacles and roadblocks that are in their way. The bigger the idea — the bigger the challenges are — and yet they don't care! In fact, they are energized by all of the problems and setbacks along the way. They're in it with all their hearts and souls and loving every minute of it! And since their game involves and demands ever-increasing amounts of money — then they are very happy when it comes rushing in!

So when you think about it <u>in</u> <u>this</u> <u>context</u>, you will quickly realize that money can and does buy these people a tremendous amount of happiness! Of course, it's the game or the hunt that they really love! The money is simply a means to that end.

<u>**Marketing:**</u> The attracting
and retaining of the very
best prospective buyers for
maximum profitability is a process
and never an event.

**You learn... grow... adapt... and
roll with the changes.**

⁓◦◦⁓

The tiger fails to catch his prey 95% of the time...

And yet <u>lives</u> <u>like</u> <u>a</u> <u>king</u> on the 5% he does catch!

❝You're never going to be a really good professional speaker until you've been in a number of really bad speaking situations.**❞**

— Jim Cathcart

- When it comes to your own personal development — it's the hard times that count the most. The good times are not that good. You must willingly put yourself through as many "<u>BAD</u>" situations as possible... to develop your skills. You gotta walk through the fire!

- Very few people actually enjoy the most difficult periods... and yet these are the times of the greatest growth. Working through these terrible times makes you stronger and wiser. It is the secret to developing yourself in the fullest way.

A simple 3-step formula to quickly develop any sales presentation:

1. Come up with your 3 BEST SELLING POINTS. What are the top 3 reasons why they must buy what you sell? What are your 3 biggest benefits that they love more than all the others? Think! Start with the longest list you can come up with and boil it down to the top three items.

2. Find and develop 3 EXCITING STORIES that help your best prospective buyers fully understand the importance of each one of your top 3 benefits. Find the stories that your best prospective buyers can relate to the most. Find the ones that specifically deal with your 3 BEST SELLING POINTS in the most powerful way. Spend some quality time working on these stories. Try to find ways to dramatize them and make them much more interesting.

3. SPECIFIC CALL TO ACTION! Create the strongest... most compelling... and most urgent reason why they must take action NOW! You must not only tell them exactly what you want them to do, but you must tell them why it is so for them to do it!

The secret to this formula comes from all the work you put into it. The more preparation, the better. The art of salesmanship is making it all sound so easy and so natural... But the secret is all the work you do to prepare in advance.

ကာ

The secret to staying young:

You don't stop playing because you grow old... You grow old because you stopped playing. SO <u>NEVER</u> STOP!

ကာ

Work in spurts!

One of the secrets to my own high level of productivity is the simple, but powerful, fact that I do most of my work in short bursts of high intensity!

I catch myself on fire... and then I burn brightly for these brief periods. The larger projects become strings of as many of these smaller pieces that are stitched together.

Are you in it to win it?

★ Or are you only playing <u>not</u> <u>to</u> <u>lose</u>?

★ Are you really going for it? Are you in it with all your heart and soul? Are you fully sold and 100% committed? Are you willing to do whatever it takes? Do you really believe that you can and will win in the biggest way?

★ If you're <u>not</u> getting the results you want or feel you could be getting — then there's a good chance that the problem is you and your level of belief, determination, commitment, and willingness to do whatever it takes (regardless of the cost) to win.

★ People who are on top of their game can easily see this and will admit to it all day long. Those who are struggling will fight the idea that they are the #1 cause of their struggle.

★ Which camp are you in? If you're a veteran, then you've probably spent a lot of time in both camps.

★ The fact that you and you alone are 100% responsible for the results you're getting is not an easy idea to accept — especially during the extremely difficult periods. But you must accept this very simple idea — if you are truly committed to achieving your biggest goals, dreams, and desires. There is no other way; stop looking for one. It does <u>not</u> exist.

Make your business a game that you play — *and then play to win!*

<u>This is much more than some silly bumper sticker idea</u>! This is a major success principle that makes you more money and lets you get more joy and satisfaction out of your business. It also makes it easier to deal with all of the adversity that hits you on a daily... weekly... monthly... and yearly basis. When you're playing a game to win — <u>you are a contender</u>! The entire purpose and meaning for why you do what you do is so much different than someone who is "trying to make a lot of money." Can you see this? I hope so!

MORE is better!

<u>Want to achieve more?</u>
Then do more! It's that simple.
Massive action is the key.
You must <u>always</u> do much more
than you think you have to do
in order to reach your goals.
Remember that.
It <u>always</u> takes more — not less —
at least in the beginning.

Mark Victor Hansen said he got rejected 144 different times before a publisher said "<u>YES!</u>" to the first *Chicken Soup for the Soul* books. <u>Now</u> <u>they've</u> <u>sold</u> <u>more</u> <u>than</u> <u>100</u> <u>million</u> <u>books</u>!

❧⊛❧

Imagine all the jealous people who say that Mark and his business partner, Jack Canfield, got lucky.

There is <u>no</u> <u>such</u> <u>thing</u> as time management!

◈ Time is like the weather... it cannot be managed or controlled. It is what it is. You have ZERO power over it.

◈ Because of this, the whole concept of "time management" is misleading and weak.

◈ A much better concept is "action management." The reason is simple: *You can control your actions!* What you decide to do at any given moment is largely within your control. And there are many things you can do to take BETTER actions that produce more of the results you want.

WAY
NUMBER
454

66Our life is frittered away
by detail... Simplify, simplify,
simplify! Simplicity of life and
the elevation of purpose.**99**

— *Henry David Thoreau*

> How many things can you live without?

> What is <u>really</u> important and what's not?

> The fewer things you want — the simpler
your life and business will be.

WAY
NUMBER
455

It's <u>NEVER</u> about the money.

The highest-qualified prospects <u>almost never</u> think about price... and when they do it's at the bottom of their list of priorities.

Most sales are lost over objections that the prospect never tells you about. They simply don't have enough confidence that your product or service is the right one for them. If it is more expensive — they are not convinced that the added advantages they will get are worth the extra money you are charging. *It's up to you to convince them!*

$\$\$\$\$\$

People will always do things for THEIR reasons — never <u>YOURS</u>!

Forget about yourself and only care about and/or communicate the things that are most important to them.

$\$\$\$\$\$

Diversity leads to stability.

Find <u>as</u> <u>many</u> <u>different</u> <u>ways</u>
as you can to get
the results you want.

MORE is better!

Find a business that can consume you!

◈ One that can fully captivate you.

◈ One that you can fall completely and totally in love with!

◈ One that will absorb you... challenge you... interest and excite you. These businesses are out there and if you can't find one – create one!

CHARGE MORE!

Are people complaining that your prices are too high? If so — DON'T LOWER THEM — just sell harder!

The fact that your prices are too high is almost never the problem. If you get this objection too much, you must ask this question: "What are you doing to prove to people — beyond any doubt — that what you offer is worth FAR MORE than the money you're asking them to give you?"

It's up to you to build the value up by educating them in every way about why you charge premium prices.

Most salespeople are so busy selling — they do not give the prospect a chance to buy! **This is no joke:**

1. They do all the talking and no listening.

2. They never engage the prospective buyer.

3. They never do the kinds of things that build trust.

4. They never give the prospect the chance to feel like they want to feel: *The most important person on earth!*

5. They never get the prospect to reveal <u>the</u> <u>real</u> <u>reasons</u> they're not buying.

It's all about the ego of the salesperson and NEVER about helping the prospect get what they want the most.

Know your limitations.

Do you?
Compensate for them in as
many ways as <u>possible</u>.

Making a lot of money is NOT about doing what you love.

It's about finding out what <u>produces</u> <u>the</u> <u>biggest</u> <u>results</u> and choosing to fall in love with those things.

Create advertising that does not look and feel like advertising.

◉ Make it look like public relations.

◉ Make it look like education.

◉ Make it look like one friend writing or communicating in some way to another friend.

◉ Make it all about them and how you can somehow give them more of what you <u>know</u> they want the most.

◉ Make it look hokey! And what is that? I'm glad you asked! Make it more fun and exciting for the people in your target market!

These are the kinds of things that will completely separate you from all of your competitors. You'll stand out... get noticed... wake the right people up... and get them involved. This of course leads them down the main path to spend more money more often in even larger amounts — while also advising all of their friends to do the same!

WAY
NUMBER
464

**Persuasion is telling someone
what to do WITHOUT actually
telling them what to do!**

- ▣ Nobody wants to be told what to do... So
  our job is to get them to do what we want
  them to do without actually telling them!

- ▣ We do <u>everything</u> <u>possible</u> to make them
  feel as if they are coming to us rather
  than us going to them.

- ▣ We make them feel as if they are the
  ones who are in power.

- ▣ We let them feel as if they are buying
  rather than us selling.

- ▣ We let them feel that spending their
  money with us is definitely in their best
  self-interest.

⚬⚬⚬

Leap without looking!

It's the entrepreneurial way.

⚬⚬⚬

❧ THE <u>DICTATOR!</u> ☙

The average customer is more demanding than ever! *More choices make them feel more empowered!*

**Throw away all of your books
on leadership. I can give all of it
to you in <u>3</u> <u>very</u> <u>simple</u> <u>words</u>:**

(Take total responsibility.)

Sound too simple? It's not. Don't let the
simplicity fool you. There is nothing
more difficult than taking complete and
total responsibility for <u>everything</u> that
happens in your life and business. *It is
the hardest thing you will ever do.* There is
so much you cannot control and yet you
must still assume total responsibility for
all of your *actions* and *reactions*.

Breaking through their self-centered fog!

All people have a very thick layer of self-centeredness that shields and protects them. Your <u>offer</u> is like the warm sun that penetrates the self-centered fog of the prospective buyer!

The problem is, the prospective buyers are moving so fast that you only have a very short amount of time for the heat of the offer to burn through their fog. You must do it fast! *What's the fastest way to do it?* Do whatever it takes to make your offer personal to them. It must speak to them in the most <u>compelling</u> and <u>direct</u> way possible or won't have time to breakthrough.

Are you focused on the obstacles *or the objectives?*

Both are important, but putting more focus on the latter will always make you more money.

One great golf shot wipes out a hundred bad ones.

<u>Stay hungry!</u>

Kids ask an average of
120 questions a day.

They are hungry!
They're curious!
They have a very powerful
need to know!
Their filters are wide open!

**But how many questions does the
<u>average</u> adult ask? SIX!!! YES,
from 120 questions a day to 6!**

*Is it any wonder why
most adults are about as creative
as a head of lettuce?*

How to double or triple your entire business... in <u>ONE</u> <u>EASY</u> <u>STEP</u>!

Just get each of your best customers to refer one other person to you who also ends up becoming a good customer and you have doubled your entire business! Get them to each refer two and your business is now 3 TIMES BIGGER and so much more profitable!

It's so simple, isn't it? YES! Of course, it's not easy — but <u>you</u> <u>can</u> <u>do</u> <u>it</u> with the right referral program that greatly rewards your customers for giving you the names and addresses (and their own endorsement) of a handful of other people they personally know and believe could greatly benefit from what you sell.

People only notice the birds with the brightest colors!

❖•❖•❖

What are you doing to get the right people to notice <u>you</u>?

Become enlightened...
◻ LIGHTEN UP! ◻

See your life and business through the eyes of a great comedy genius. Your most creative ideas will only come to you when you are totally fired up! You can't be too serious... *Do whatever it takes, each day, to lighten up!*

What do you say when you've already said everything you have to say a million times?

Answer: Say it 1,000,001 times!

Lesson: The customers will NEVER get tired of hearing good sales pitch stories that excite them and offer them something they badly want. Just because you're sick and tired of telling these sales stories to them does <u>not</u> mean that they are tired of hearing them.

Are you cheating?

- People laugh when I tell them that I write the same sales letter over and over again. They think it's a joke. And once they realize that I'm not joking — they think I'm doing something wrong! I'm not. All I am doing is being creative!

- *There is nothing worse than the blank screen or page!* Having very good models that you can take ideas from is the fun and creative part of producing sales material that sells!

- This is a MAJOR shortcut! It is a faster and easier way to write the very best sales letters you can possibly write. You'll get a greater abundance of powerful selling ideas you can work with — and if you start with the best models — those ideas will be much more powerful.

- Creating new sales material from a pile of existing material is what creativity is all about!

⤢⟶⟵⤣

Success comes from
self-discipline.

So does real self-esteem! Those who want
more self-esteem must do more esteemable
activities more often! It's as simple as that.
Self-discipline is all about forcing yourself to do
the most important things you know you must
do (but often don't feel like doing).

⤢⟶⟵⤣

If you do what everyone
else is doing — you're going
to get the results that
everyone else is getting...
which are average, <u>at</u> <u>best</u>.

If you want extraordinary results you MUST do extraordinary things!

The ugly truth...

Even the most honest people
— with the highest of all
integrity — still think it's okay
to lie to a salesperson.

THOUGHT JOGGERS:

What are your top five greatest selling messages?

Why should they buy from <u>YOU</u> and not someone else?

What are the strongest inducements that will make them buy right now?

- *The best offer?*

- *The best bribe?*

What is the <u>strongest</u> <u>and</u> <u>most</u> <u>believable</u> reason to get them to send you their money right away?

The Killer Marketer:

We smell blood
every time one of our
promotions works...
And we only want more!

How To Create Your Marketing System:

1. You find out what works best (through testing).

2. Then you expand those activities as far as possible. You do more testing to discover *"how high is high?"*

3. Then you <u>focus</u> on the areas that bring you the best results. You create procedures that do those things automatically.

≥⟨W⟩≤

Most managers...
are not demanding enough from their people and holding them accountable. This is especially true with huge companies.

Someone once told me the story of a wealthy land owner who called in one of his employees and said, "I've been reviewing the employee records and see you've been working here for 25 years to take care of our stables. Is that right?" The employee said, "YES!" And the owner replied, "But we sold all of our horses off 20 years ago. Isn't that correct?" And the employee said, "Yes, that's right, sir, and what would you like for me to do next?"

This may be a joke, but if you've been around business for a while, you instantly see the truth in this! *Most employees will do whatever you ask them to do – and nothing more.*

Making money
and keeping it are
<u>two</u> <u>entirely</u>
<u>different</u> <u>things</u>.

❧

Both require
unique strategies.

Nine Essentials You Need to Know to Market Your Business.

by Misty Williams

Your chances for business success increase exponentially when you clearly understand the most important **essentials** for growing your business:

1. Know what you do best. 2. Know who your customers are. 3. Know how customers find you. 4. Know your "sales process." 5. Know where you add the most value. 6. Know your competitive business advantages. 7. Know where to spend your money. 8. Know the most painful and weakest areas of your business. 9. Know when to look for help.

❦

How can you improve in all nine
of these vital areas?
Where is your strongest and weakest link?

Great sales copy goes *straight* to the emotions!

- It's human warmth on paper!

- It's one-to-one personal communication.

- It's you and me sitting down face-to-face and having a warm heart-to-heart talk about a product or service that can truly help you.

- It must reek of sincerity.

❖ ❖ ❖

A closer's secret:
Have complete disregard
for anything but the money!

❖ ❖ ❖

✿

Only an entrepreneur can understand another entrepreneur.

Team dynamics from one of the world's greatest basketball coaches:

❝ They said you have to use your five best players, but I found you win with the five who fit together the best. ❞

— Red Auerbach
(9-Time NBA Champion as a Coach and
7-Time Champion as a General Manager)

—◦◦◦—

You never get what you want — you only get what you expect!

High expectation is
the key to taking your
business to the next level.

—◦◦◦—

A few words about consultants:

- It's <u>always</u> easy to give advice from a safe port.

- Just like it's <u>always</u> so much easier to take risks with someone else's money.

Don't be scammed!

Nobody has all the answers...
no matter how good they may be at
fooling people into believing so.

((∞))

<u>Game</u> <u>Theory</u> <u>for</u> <u>Marketers:</u>

"Game Theory" is the latest buzz of the academic community. Highly educated people have made quite a study of this new area. The concept is simple: "Put yourself into a position that you <u>don't</u> want to be in and then rescue yourself!" In the process of doing this, you discover <u>many</u> interesting things. When I first read about this I said to myself, "This is what all great entrepreneurs have been doing since the beginning of time!" *It's true!* We constantly force ourselves to tap into parts of ourselves that we don't normally reach by constantly biting off way more than we can chew! We back ourselves into corners and then <u>fight</u> <u>our</u> <u>way</u> <u>out!</u>

There is **so much joy**
that comes from the long-term
effects of a life of hard work,
discipline, focus, goal setting,
commitment, and daily striving
to work towards your dream.

Put yourself through more pressure... <u>every</u> <u>day</u>!

♛

Pressure changes everything! It is the amazing energy you need to perform at your highest level!

❖ ❖ ❖

A confession and a lesson.

- My first couple of years in sales were a disaster... one sales job after another... always in the bottom group.

- I'd have enough good days to keep me excited about the idea of being a salesperson, but there were plenty of days when it was <u>nothing</u> <u>but</u> <u>frustration</u>.

- Then in December of 1985 I started my first company and my ability to sell instantly and dramatically increased! All of a sudden, I got a lot better — fast!

- *What was it that created this sudden difference?* Simple. All of a sudden, I was selling something I really believed in!

Spend less, invest more!

Stop blowing your money on all kinds of worthless CRAP and <u>start</u> <u>investing</u> <u>it</u> in things that stand the greatest chance of making you the maximum amount of money.

Expect MORE!

Our expectations tend to be self-fulfilling.

In other words — <u>we</u> <u>get</u> <u>what</u> <u>we</u> <u>expect</u>.

The more you realize this great truth, the BIGGER your expectations will be!

Getting old sucks! Except for one really cool thing:

Having the ability to reflect.

...It's a powerful thing!

It is great to have gained enough <u>personal</u> <u>experiences</u> to be able to look back and see things from your past that enable you to make the RIGHT CHOICES today.

Money and success and all the trappings are important, but...

In the end, it's not the material shit that matters... It's not the money you've accumulated. It's the way you've lived your life... Did you do what you wanted? Did you experience love? Did you care about something passionately? Take risks? Were you trying to get the most out of your life? Were you surrounded by the things you loved? Did you connect with yourself? Love yourself? Get to know yourself? Did you surround yourself with a life filled with things that were satisfying to you? Did you love your work? Really love it? Was it fulfilling? Challenging? Interesting to you? Did you put your entire being into it? Did you use your talents? Face your fears? Grow and develop? Care deeply about someone and something other than yourself? Did you question your life? And question your place in it? Did you think for yourself or blindly follow others? Did you dare to be great? Did you go for the gold? Were you willing to think big? Risk big? Work hard?

Work passionately? Did you seek the truth?
Were you curious? What did you do with
that curiosity? What were your biggest
interests and desires? What did you do to
fulfill your passions?

The world of business can be a great vehicle
for doing all these things. **But it's got to be
about more than just the money.**